CANCELLED

CANCELLED

CANCELLED

ENGLAND'S HERO
WAYNE ROONEY

Sue Evison

JOHN BLAKE

CANCELLED

C 35030

CITY OF LIMERICK PUBLIC LIBRARY

922

96334

Published by John Blake Publishing Ltd,
3, Bramber Court, 2 Bramber Road,
London W14 9PB, England

www.blake.co.uk

First published in paperback in 2004

ISBN 1 84454 090 1

All rights reserved. No part of this publication may be reproduced,
stored in a retrieval system, or in any form or by any means, without
the prior permission in writing of the publisher, nor be otherwise
circulated in any form of binding or cover other than that in which it is
published and without a similar condition including this condition
being imposed on the subsequent publisher.

British Library Cataloguing-in-Publication Data:

A catalogue record for this book is available from the British Library.

Design by www.envydesign.co.uk

Printed in Great Britain by CPD

1 3 5 7 9 10 8 6 4 2

© Text copyright Sue Evison

Picture credits
Pictures reproduced by kind permission of News Group Newspapers,
Liverpool Daily Post and Echo and PA Photos

Papers used by John Blake Publishing are natural, recyclable
products made from wood grown in sustainable forests.
The manufacturing processes conform to the environmental
regulations of the country of origin.

*To Jasper, the best son in the world,
and my exceptional mother, Irene*

ACKNOWLEDGEMENTS

The author would like to record her grateful thanks and appreciation to all of the people who have helped in the writing of this biography.

I am particularly grateful, of course, to Wayne Rooney and his fiancée Coleen McLoughlin, for being there and being themselves and to the people of Liverpool for their good humour and help.

A special 'thank you' to Mike Parry for his wonderful Foreword, Lucian Randall at Blake Publishing. For additional research and advice, thanks to Chris Jones and Mike Cavenett.

For their encouragement, help, understanding and support, I'd also like to thank Rebekah Wade, Geoff Webster, Fergus Shanahan, John Blake, Michelle Signore, Rosie Ries, Ben Jackson, Graham Dudman, Phil Thomas, Derek Brown, Jimmy Clarke, Dan Kennedy, Max Clifford, Mark Borkowski, Bronwen Andrews, Julia Hosp, Nigel Bentley, Tim Redsell, Nigel Gordon-Stewart, Jane Atkinson and The Cat, Nancy Hesketh, Louis Wood and all at News International from library to legal.

CONTENTS

FOREWORD

NEVER IN THE field of football conflict has one man so dominated the course of international competition as Wayne Rooney did at Euro 2004. With him, England were simply unstoppable. He was a goal machine, creating and scoring in equal measure.

Without him, as he was cruelly cut down in the quarter-final against Portugal, a vacuum opened up at the heart of the England team which was ruthlessly exploited by the opposition. The Portuguese knew that, in removing Rooney, they were taking the firing chamber out of a Gatling gun.

Rooney's true arrival on the international stage came in the seventieth minute of the opening game in France as the Merseyside protégé turned the Gallic defence upside-down and headed single-mindedly in the only direction he knows on the compass – GW – goalwards.

The crowd noise rose through a rumble to a roar as he

shrugged off three defenders and moved into the area. He had made himself at least two yards in which to shoot and he raised his lethal right foot as he prepared to pull the trigger. Then, in an act of shameless cynicism, French defender Mikael Silvestre swept Rooney's legs away, a foul for which he certainly should have been sent off.

Nevertheless, the man who had just become the youngest ever player to appear in the finals of this competition had provided England with the means to double their 1–0 advantage over the French and secure us a certain victory.

Had we known then what we know now, the Everton boy who was wearing the legendary England number nine shirt should have taken the penalty. His ability to play in front of 65,000 people as though he was back in his school playground gave him an advantage that didn't belong to any of the other 21 professionals on the pitch, aching and agitated at the drama unfolding in front of them in the 100°F heat.

But there were no big thinkers in the dug-out that day. The coach and his support squad knew that Captain Fantastic, David Beckham, was struggling both mentally and physically. But he is England's penalty-taker and you could hardly blame him for assuming it was his kick.

He was thwarted by a brilliant save from the often clown-like Fabien Barthez. We would have needed a crystal ball then to comprehend the cost of that miss.

But the wasted penalty opportunity was not the most salient point of those five dramatic minutes. As the incident was played over and over again on the giant screens in the stadium, on the Jumbotrons in the centre of the Portuguese capital and on television screens from Rio to Rochdale via Ayers Rock, millions of fans were muttering one word to each other, 'R-O-O-N-E-Y'. Claxon horns were sounding around the world.

I was sitting very close to the pitch on that incredible evening, just a few rows back, and was able to study at very close hand the way Rooney went forward. He moved through the French defence with balletic grace. He has this gift to be able to keep his head up and weigh up his options while his feet are performing the sort of tricks we last saw in *The Lord of The Rings*.

Though this was the first time he was taking on France's former World Cup-winning defence, they had seen enough of him for the previous 70 minutes to know that, if they let him get into the penalty area, he would find a hole the size of the Channel Tunnel to exploit their disarray. I saw three French defenders all screaming at each other as the crowd noise was rising to a frenzy. And, of course, as the floodlights burned down from the roof of the stadium, giving Rooney a shadow in all four directions, they didn't know which one to chase.

Ecstasy turned to agony at the penalty miss but those around me couldn't stop talking about the move that brought it about. For my own part, I couldn't get overexcited. It was not that I wasn't mightily impressed by a display of football skill that you might only see perhaps two or three times in a season. It was not that, as an Evertonian, my heart wasn't bursting with pride that the club I had supported all my life, that my father and grandfather had supported, had produced one of the greatest players we are ever likely to see.

It was just that I had been so expectant that the moment I had just witnessed was always going to come. If anything, I was a little questioning that three-quarters of the game had gone before Wayne had produced his ultimate moment of magic. There had been plenty of hints throughout the match that he was capable of something special, but now, for all to see, he had produced it.

I so wish he had not been taken off very shortly afterwards, because students of Rooneyism knew then, as tens of millions know now, that when something good happens something better always follows. We'll never know if Wayne would have rescued the team from the penalty miss but, when you look at how the rest of the competition went, you would be mad to have bet against it.

He certainly would have been Man of the Match, as he was in the two following group games, had it not been for the fact that the remarkable Zinedine Zidane scored twice in the dying minutes of the game to snatch victory for his nation.

My own satisfaction came from the fact that I had already warned the nation what to expect.

I had been asked to write a series of features on Euro 2004 for a group of evening newspapers across the country, which included publications in the football hot-bed areas of Liverpool, Newcastle and the West Midlands.

In the first piece I wrote on Wednesday, 8 June, I didn't bother previewing the respective merits of the 16 nations involved, I simply stated, 'Whatever happens to England in Euro 2004, one thing is for certain: Wayne Rooney will emerge at the other end of the competition as one of the greatest footballers in the world. To those who have not so far been party to his range of talents he will easily be the discovery of the tournament.

'In a month's time, the football world will be in a frenzy as he becomes the hottest property on the planet in a pair of football boots.'

My brash and seemingly outrageous prediction provoked comment and derision from every quarter. One e-mail sent to me read, 'Whilst I admire your faith in a young England player, do you really expect us to believe that this kid, who has scored four goals for Everton in the Premiership this season, is going to outshine the Henrys and even the Ronaldos of this world?'

Others were far less considerate. One communication stated, 'Blue-tinted glasses are one thing, but trying to wind up the nation that in young Wayne Rooney we have a world-beater is irresponsible to both the lad and the expectations of millions of fans.'

I never had the slightest doubt.

The doubters, though, weren't confined to the ranks of the general population, many of whom may not have the experience to know any better. Let's just dwell for a moment on the attitude of a former England captain towards the boy-man who is now regarded as our most influential player.

Rooney arrived in Portugal on the back of a brace of

goals against Iceland. OK, so it was only a warm-up game against one of the smallest countries in the world, but it is great for the morale of any striker to be hitting the back of the net.

For some reason, though, this did not make Tony Adams, the hugely distinguished Arsenal and England leader, a very happy man. His advice – and, remember, Adams is now a manager in his own right at Wycombe Wanderers – was that Rooney was not worth his place in the starting line-up. He didn't think that the Everton striker and Liverpool's Michael Owen would work together, so Rooney would have to go.

You could say that this was fair comment, because, after all, none of us had seen him in the heat of competitive battle and I accepted that, while I *knew* Rooney would get the better of any defence he was up against, not everybody was as well acquainted with his talents as me.

But, after the French game, Adams wrote again that Rooney should not start the following game. What flaws in the Croxteth kid's game had Adams spotted that had passed the rest of us by? French defenders were queuing up to tell their own journalists how glad they were that Rooney had been taken off when he was, because they were terrified of him.

The story gets more bizarre. When Wayne scored his two against Switzerland in the hottest football stadium I have ever been to, he, of course, achieved instant world stardom. It was fair to say that he had proved a point. The doubters had become believers; the intrigued had become mouth-dribbling devotees.

CITY OF LIMERICK
PUBLIC LIBRARY

But there was still one man in the world who couldn't see what all the fuss was about. Believe it or not, Tony Adams went to print and *again* urged that Wayne should be dropped for the forthcoming Croatia game. His bizarre reasoning was that Rooney 'gets in the way of Michael Owen scoring goals'.

The boy with feet that move faster than the pistons on a steam engine naturally made nonsense of Adams's rantings by going on to score another brace against the Croats. I don't know whether Adams gave up doubting Rooney at that point, or whether or not the publication for which he was writing was just too embarrassed to keep publishing.

What a privilege it was to be present in the stadiums at the birth of a superstar.

The only game that England played outside the capital, Lisbon, was the second group game against Switzerland in a dusty little town 100 miles north called Coimbra. It's a nice enough little venue, though the authorities didn't have time to finish it off and there's only a partial roof at one end, exposing the fans to furnace-like heat. It was a 5.00pm kick-off, so there was no respite from the sun.

The team came out in their training gear about 20 minutes before the kick-off to warm up under coach Sammy Lee, formerly the Liverpool trainer who is now full-time at the FA. I watched intently as Wayne went through his paces. He seemed to want to specialise in striking long balls. He would get somebody to deliver him a ball from afar and then, with barely one touch, he would control it and whip it back.

But, as he did so, he seemed to lean and spin on the turn, giving the effect that he was always hitting the ball on the half-volley.

From the first whistle, he was involved everywhere. Just as he had done against France, he was chasing back and harrying the Swiss midfield. It was also obvious that he was developing a relationship with Michael Owen. And it was his Merseyside team-mate who provided him with his first goal.

After 23 minutes, Owen found himself surrounded by defenders on the edge of the area. But, intelligent as he is, he saw the smallest of openings and scooped a ball over into the middle. As Wayne said later, 'I couldn't miss.' He leaped like a salmon and used every last neck muscle to power a header into the roof of the net.

I only saw him heading upwards. Every spectator in the stadium leaped to their feet and, through a tiny gap around a hundred heads, I saw the youngest ever scorer in the competition cart-wheeling away to the corner flag.

I knew then that it was only a question of time before he scored again. Sure enough, after three-quarters of the game he found himself in space and, as he says, 'I hit it as hard as I could.' It flew towards the far left-hand bottom corner of the goal, and pinballed its way into the net. And I couldn't help noticing he'd hit it with that turning and falling action I'd seen earlier during the pre-match warm-up.

A friend of mine from the Press Association tried to rain on Wayne's parade. They marked the strike down as an own goal on the basis that the ball hit the upright and the back of the goalkeeper's head before crossing the line.

What an absolute load of rubbish. An own goal is when a ball that is not going in the direction of the back of the net is suddenly diverted by a member of the opposing team and ends up crossing the line. Fortunately, UEFA took no notice of the PA's view and the goal was duly credited to the hero of the night.

The world has changed many times for Wayne in the months since Euro 2004 but, for me, the biggest change of all came in the aftermath of this game. Though England's youngest had never had any doubt about his own ability, he now realised that he had well and truly arrived on the world stage.

Immediately following international football matches, there is a system behind the scenes called 'the Mixed Zone'. After years of wrangling between the football authorities and the increasing numbers of the media, it was designed as a forum to try and bring together players and those who wished to interview them.

It works a bit like the system you see at an airport, when famous people are coming through Arrivals and everybody else is penned behind a fence as they pass by. To leave the ground and get to their coach, the footballers and managers have to pass through the Mixed Zone. Reporters and interviewers either side will call out for them to stop and talk.

A radio broadcaster might want to try and grab a few words for his outstretched mini-disc, while a group of pressmen are seeking the views on a member of the opposition about a controversial incident. The beauty of the system is that it is at the total discretion of the individual player as to whether they stop or not.

Very few of us at that stage had even heard Wayne Rooney speak. That is no exaggeration. Within the previous 90 minutes, he had become the most famous footballer in the world and yet most of us didn't have a clue what he sounded like.

We had been told that he was a shy, nervous kid, slightly in awe of the fuss that he was creating, who just liked to do his job and slip away at the end of the game. Well, if that had been the case, that image disappeared for ever in the aftermath of Switzerland.

In the same way that he often seems reluctant to make a great fuss when he scores a goal, he certainly didn't waltz though the Mixed Zone inviting attention. But, when a crescendo of requests to talk was hurled at him, he good-naturedly agreed and, for the first time, the voice of Wayne Rooney started reverberating around the planet.

Far from being shy, he was confident. He was witty and good humoured, full of praise for his team-mates and completely underwhelmed by all the attention.

Of course, the exploits in Coimbra had whetted the appetite of the England fans who were now, to a man and a woman, fully paid-up members of the Rooney-Looney Army.

An interesting aspect of the mass popularity of the boy is that his total and universal appeal could never have happened if he had been on the books of Manchester United, Liverpool, Arsenal or Chelsea.

There is tremendous angst between the fans of the two North-West giants and similar growing bitterness between the London clubs. And it has always been down to the fact that southern clubs badly resent the success of northern teams and vice versa.

Sadly for Evertonians, the blue team on Merseyside are regarded as little threat to anybody challenging for honours in the game and, therefore, the 60,000 England fans in Portugal were delighted to be able to regard the new national hero as a 'neutral'. At each stadium we went to, there were thousands of flags from supporters' clubs all over the country.

And, no matter who they were supporting back home, they now broke into the chant of 'ROONEY … ROONEY' at every available opportunity. This was because they saw no disloyalty in pinning their colours to the mast of a player whose team was unlikely to do them very much harm the following season.

The third group game was back in the Stadium of Light in Lisbon. The night before the game, my hotel was full of Croatian fans and officials and there was only one subject they wanted to know about. I did my job for England by supplying them with a plethora of false information.

I told them all that Rooney was stronger with his left foot than his right, that he had won the English schools 100m championship in an Olympic qualifying time and that he had been banned from ever taking part in boxing again because his last opponent had spent three months in a coma after he had felled him in the first round.

With each lurid fact, the faces of the Croatians

became more and more strained. I told them that scientific tests had proved that Rooney had a bigger brain than Einstein. It took Einstein years to develop the theory of relativity, but it only takes the boy genius a split-second to work out how to turn and place a ball in the perfect spot to score a goal.

Just before half-time in the Croatia game the following day, the Einstein theory seemed to come true. England were trailing from an early goal. But, five minutes before half-time, Wayne found himself in possession 12 yards out. He spotted Scholes in a better position and instantly flicked the ball on.

The Manchester United midfielder duly finished it off and got the monkey off his back for not having scored for England for three years. One could have assumed that, as this was the 41st minute, we would go in at half-time all square. England's centre-forward had other ideas.

Buoyed on by the equaliser, England surged forward again. Scholes squared it to Rooney and instinct took over. Without even checking his pace, he cracked the ball in the direction of the far post. I was sitting at the opposite end of the stadium directly in line with the striker and his target. As soon as he made contact with the ball, I could see where it was going. I was out of my seat a good two seconds before anybody else in the stadium. It flew in like an arrow. The goalkeeper did get a despairing touch on it, but there was so much power in the shot that he might as well have been trying to swat away an incoming Trident missile.

I didn't realise it, but at that point I was in tears of

ecstasy. Nobody was ever going to be able to say now that his earlier performances were a one-off. This boy was a goal-machine. I'd been shouting it from the rooftops of the football communities of the world telling everybody what was to come – and it was all happening.

In the second half, I was lucky enough to be sitting right behind the goal where Wayne scored his second. Some would say it was the goal of the tournament. He played the one-two with Michael Owen and then moved forward like a relentless predator.

The Croatian defence desperately tried to catch him. I kept urging him to shoot before he was hauled down in the area, knowing he would probably not take the spot-kick. But he held it and held it for what seemed like an eternity, before so casually sliding it home.

Talking again after the game, it was clear that he had formulated his own plan. The Croatian goalkeeper believed he had it covered because 'keepers believe that they can tell where a forward is going to slot the ball by reading their eyes. Unfortunately, Wayne has already mastered the trick of completely confusing the last line of defence by usually looking one way and placing the ball the other.

David Seaman, in fact, said after the game that Wayne had fooled him in exactly the same way when he scored the Premiership goal in October 2002 that first brought him to the attention of the world. Rooney had literally plucked the ball out of the air with his right foot, brought it to ground and was advancing on Seaman's goal. The Arsenal defence backed off. After all, what could this diminutive 16-year-old kid, who had just come on as substitute, do from 20 yards out against England's number 1?

Meanwhile, Seaman started to get alarmed. He saw an intent in the way the sandy-haired kid was moving towards him and saw him weighing up the far corner. He looked to his top left. Should he commit himself? A split-second later, it was irrelevant. Rooney had struck the ball towards the other side of the goal. The ball had soared over Seaman, dipped and then crashed over the line from the underside of the bar. Goodison Park erupted and nobody who was there that day will ever forget the look of bewilderment on the faces of the Arsenal defence who had been slain by a force that nobody quite yet understood.

The three group games in Portugal had proved with mounting certainty just how valuable Wayne Rooney had become to our international set-up. Confidence ahead of the quarter-final tie against hosts Portugal was immense. But, unfortunately, we were about to have to address a situation that none of us saw coming.

Our assumption was that providing Sven picked Rooney – which, of course, now went without saying – then the rest of the game-plan was to make sure that every move was designed to feed the ball to him in order that he could go about his lethal business.

So you can imagine the shockwaves that reverberated around the Stadium of Light when we saw this figure hobbling around without a boot. At first, we thought it was just a simple matter of losing the boot in the previous scramble with the Portuguese defender, Andrade. But then he got it back and he struggled to put it on.

When he did, it was obvious he couldn't walk. His actions to deflect the pain were so obvious that I knew instinctively that he had had it. He sat spread-eagled on the turf and he knew his tournament was over. He tried to hobble for a few minutes but it was hopeless.

The first word that came back from the dressing room was that he had twisted an ankle. Immense relief. But a few minutes later, we learned that he had been taken to hospital for an X-ray. Eventually, the news that he had a broken metatarsal filtered through.

It was the strangest sort of injury because, to all intents and purposes, it looked like he had been kicked from behind by Jorge Andrade and that that's why his boot had been prised off. But the referee decided that Rooney was at fault and penalised him for it. By some strange medical riddle, a kick in the back of the foot resulted in a broken bone at the front of the foot – apparently due to the pressure of the boot before it flew off.

The inquest could go on for ever. The point was that Wayne would take no more part in the competition.

An indication of England's reliance on their centre-forward was that, as soon as he left the field, nobody knew what to do. Should Paul Scholes have been pushed up into a slot similar to Rooney's to support Michael Owen? Should substitute Darius Vassell have been told to try and imitate the Rooney role or should Sven have reshuffled the whole game-plan to defend our early Michael Owen lead?

Actually, nothing happened and, as the game wore on, the familiar sight of long balls being lobbed over the

Portuguese defence for Michael Owen to run on to became a regular but unfulfilling feature.

The rest is history. We lost the penalty shoot-out.

We will never know what would have happened if Rooney had stayed on the pitch. But, on the evidence of the first three games and the fact that, ultimately, Portugal were not good enough to win the tournament on their own turf, we have to assume that one-man-Wayne could have made a difference.

I am certain that, if he had been involved in a penalty shoot-out, he would never have missed.

There is no point in speculating where Rooney goes from here. It doesn't matter who he plays for or what shirt he is wearing; he is going to be one of the great footballers of all time. He will be the greatest English footballer we have ever seen and his influence will circumnavigate the world.

Throughout Euro 2004, I wore a metal badge on my shirt. It has a picture of Wayne Rooney and the lettering around his head says 'England's youngest player'.

At the start of the tournament, people would point at my badge and ask me why I was wearing it and my answer was, 'Because he's going to be the greatest player you have ever seen.'

I also had a tremendous stroke of luck earlier this year. I was informed by one of the charities to whom Wayne gives his time (and his boots and shirts) that a special shirt was being auctioned at a dinner in the Midlands.

The shirt was, in fact, the one worn by Wayne when he made his England début as the youngest ever player to turn out for his country. It was against Australia at Upton Park in February 2003.

I was asked by the benefactors, the people from RMCC, a charity backed by McDonald's, who provide rooms and flats at hospitals for parents who want to be near their very sick children, whether I was going to bid.

Though I would love to have acquired the shirt – because I realised, in years to come, it was going to be one of the outstanding pieces of football memorabilia of all time – I didn't think I had any chance at all of being able to afford such a coveted treasure. The dinner was being attended by people from the world of showbusiness, politics and the City and I figured that it would be snapped up by somebody whose budget was a thousand times what I had to spend.

Nevertheless, I arranged for a bidder to go on my behalf with very strict instructions as to what I could afford.

Astonishingly, I outbid everybody else and the shirt was mine. I was so pleased when I went to pick it up that I wrote out another cheque for what I hope was a generous donation to the charity.

I was in awe as it was handed over. England were playing in red that night. There is the number 9 figure on the front and, embroidered into the shirt in white cotton, are the words 'England v Australia, February 22, 2003'. Above this, written in black felt-tip pen, is the inscription 'Very Best Wishes – Wayne Rooney'.

During the course of the competition in Portugal, as Wayne's fame and reputation was growing and growing, I was reflecting one evening on my shirt. It had been beautifully folded up into a silver frame and was hanging proudly on my living-room wall in my home in Epsom.

Later that night, I suddenly awoke with a start in my bed. While I was away at the Championships, I was having a new bathroom fitted at home. Several groups of workmen had keys to my house.

Now don't get me wrong – they are honourable artisans and craftsmen, as honest as the day is long. But just supposing, while their back was turned, or they were taking in a delivery of tiles or off-loading a bath from a lorry, an interloper should suddenly enter my house looking for something valuable.

I broke into a sweat. 'That's the most valuable football shirt in the world,' I had convinced myself. If it gets nicked, I have lost everything worth having in life. They can have the house but not my Wayne Rooney shirt.

As dawn broke the next morning, I was on the phone to my solicitor back in Surrey. He must have thought I was mad, but I asked him to go around to my place double quick and take possession of the shirt.

It is now stored in a strongroom in a lawyer's office in stockbroker belt, Surrey.

I will never part with it.

Mike Parry,
TalkSPORT Breakfast Show Presenter
and Lifelong Everton Supporter

ALL I ever wanted to do was walk out at Goodison Park with our theme tune, Z-Cars, playing in the background. I wanted it so much … As a kid, I used to get shivers down my spine when I heard it and I still do TODAY.

1

CHILD'S PLAY

THE BALL THUDDED against the pebbledashed wall, slivers of dusty paint exploding from its impact on the terraced house as a familiar cry echoed from within: 'WA-AYNE,' the voice yelled, as an irate woman bustled out of the door, wagging her finger at the plump, broad-shouldered lad standing sheepishly in the drizzling rain, the ball clutched protectively behind his back. He knew he was in for a slap, but it never stopped him.

Instinct urged him on, the magic in his feet casting its spell as the engrossed six-year-old aimed shot after shot at the makeshift goal in the garden of his grandma's council house.

The boy had a dream and had already etched his future into the paintwork of his bedroom window overlooking a jaded suburban street in Liverpool — 'Rooney, W ... EFC' it read.

But as he carefully scratched his yearning into the splintered wooden surround, the little boy could never have imagined how quickly his dream would come true.

Today, Wayne Rooney is a world megastar, an Everton and England hero and, to some, including pop star Robbie Williams, 'simply a god'.

He may be just 18 years old, but he's been called a genius, likened to legendary footballer Pele – by the man himself – and described by England's former goalgetter Gary Lineker as 'potentially the best England player of my lifetime'.

For good measure, Lineker adds, 'It beggars belief a kid could be as good as him.'

Wayne understands exactly how he feels, because he's still pinching himself, too.

'Just a year ago, I couldn't have dreamed this,' he says. 'When I look back, I can hardly believe it. It sometimes feels a bit mad to be regarded as England's centre-forward when I've just had my eighteenth birthday.

'It's the sort of thing you pretend to be when you're a kid, knocking a ball about in the street.'

These days, Wayne has already attracted mutterings from neighbours at his posh new £900,000 mansion in Liverpool's upmarket Formby, by belting a ball noisily and repeatedly against a wall.

Old habits die hard, and Wayne picked his up as a small boy on frequent visits to the home of his gran Mavis, a few doors away from the three-bedroom council house where he grew up in the tough Merseyside district of Croxteth.

Gran Mavis was a rock for Wayne's parents in

turbulent times. His dad, also called Wayne, was a hod-carrier, jobbing as a casual labourer on building sites. Work was scarce and frequent spells of unemployment left a legacy of determination that the same fate would not befall his sons.

Mum Jeanette worked at two jobs to make ends meet, by day as a dinner lady at the all-boys De La Salle Roman Catholic High School, where Wayne would later become a pupil, and by night as a cleaner at the all-girls St John Bosco Roman Catholic High school nearby.

Wayne and his two brothers Graham, 15, and John, 13, often stayed with their grandma while their parents struggled to make ends meet.

A doughty, no-nonsense woman, gran Mavis helped keep the lads on the straight and narrow, dishing out a clip round the ear when they strayed out of line and soothing words, accompanied by a sticky Everton mint, when the world seemed glaringly unjust.

Wayne was an unassuming boy, quiet and shy. But, even back then, he smouldered with a steadily burning desire, one which urged him out of bed into the crisp morning light to conjure up the magic in his feet.

While others slept, the determined boy would sneak outside at 7.00am, often alone except for his scuffed football, and zealously practise his shots, waking the neighbours and leaving his exasperated gran to tear after him before another area of paint and render was blasted off her wall.

'Nan didn't think it was funny,' says Wayne. 'She'd hear the pebbles fall from the wall and yell, "WA-AYNE!" and I'd get a clip but I'd still be there first thing in the morning, just kicking the ball over and over. I remember the first time I kicked a ball around the garden at five years old – I've wanted to play ever since.

'The feeling of scoring a goal, even when you were a little boy, was amazing. Once I started scoring, I didn't want to stop.'

His cousin Thomas, 19, himself a promising footballer who has just signed to Macclesfield, was one of the close-knit circle who shared scraped knees and cuffed ears with Wayne as he surged his way through childhood. He says, 'Whatever we did we did together – me, Wayne and our cousin Stephen, who we call Gilly – usually. Sometimes it would be me or Gilly that would mess up the wall, but we'd tell Nan it was Wayne – he never split.

'We had one game which we played in the street where two people cross and the 'keeper has to catch five headers or volleys to come out of goal. Wayne was good at that – even in goal. He could make it there as well if ever they needed an emergency 'keeper … he's boss.'

When the boys grew old enough to venture outside the back garden, they made the Bowlie their new stadium – a rough, postage-stamp of grass which had once been a bowling green before it was trampled under the eager feet of Wayne's gang and others before them.

If their pitch became too swampy, deluged by relentless rain which drove other souls to seek the warmth of their homes, the boys simply retreated to the street, using sweaters and crumpled Coke cans to mark out the goalmouth.

Says Wayne, 'It didn't matter where we were, what

the weather was like, nothing stopped us playing football. Even when we went on holiday to the caravan park in Wales, we'd find a gang and arrange a game.

'We'd come home from primary school and we'd get changed and go straight out in the garden, usually with my friends Bradley and John, who I'm still in touch with.

'We used to put our coats down as goalposts and pretend to be our heroes – I was always Gazza, Alan Shearer or Duncan Ferguson.

'I remember scoring my first goal in the playground – it was brilliant, everybody ran over and congratulated me. It was such an amazing feeling – as soon as I scored I felt like I was on top of the world. It's still like that now.

'If it wasn't football, I'd be playing Mutant Ninja Teenage Turtles – I was mad about the Turtles, we all were at school. We used to wrap our ties round our heads and pretend to be ninjas, throwing each other down on to the floor and doing all the ninja moves – I was always Rafael, he was my favourite.

'I also had a mountain bike as a kid and rollerblades – mine were navy-blue and we used to think we looked really cool with those on with our tracky bottoms, blading around the streets – I was quite good!'

Wayne was close to his gran Mavis – and devastated when she died in 2001. He said, 'When I was 13, my granddad Rick died from lung cancer. I was very close to my nan and I started to stay with her a lot.

'She'd give me a clip round the ear and go mad at me if I did something wrong – I always deserved it when she did – but when I did something well she'd buy me a football kit.

'I played pranks on her, like putting salt or pepper in her tea, but I felt close to her. I'd pop round and make her a cup of tea and sit and watch the TV with her, usually *Prisoner Cell Block H*, her favourite programme.

'Then she got ill, too, also with lung cancer. I'd begged them both to give up smoking and also my mum – she did after Nan died but recently started again and I nag her every day.

'While Nan was ill, I used to stay over. I'd go and get her shopping from Kwiksave, walking there and taking a taxi back, and help round the house with cleaning and the like.

'When she died, I was devastated – obviously, I loved her. At her funeral, I was going to carry her coffin but instead I wrote a speech and read it out to everyone. I'd never spoken in public before, it was hard, but I wanted to do it for my nan.

'I was just in the Everton youth team when she died, so she never got to see me play in the Premiership or for England. It's my one regret, that she didn't get to see me play for England, but I think she'd be proud of me. I still think about her every day and visit her grave, to lay flowers. She was like my rock.'

A passion for soccer – and boxing – ran in the veins of the Rooney clan who had enjoyed low-wattage sporting success before Wayne blew the fuse and electrified the world with his brilliance.

Wayne's dad showed world-class promise as a boxer before injury cut short his career. He is a Lancashire champion and also boxed for England as an amateur.

Cousin Thomas was himself an English schools

boxing champion before the siren call of soccer proved too great, and Wayne's brother, Graham, gave up a place at Everton's Youth Academy to box, competing regularly for Croxteth Amateur Boxing Club at Everton Park Sports Centre.

Wayne's youngest brother, John, is content to follow in his famous sibling's footsteps. He's on the books at Everton Youth Academy, too, and, like Wayne before him, is often egged on from the sidelines by his uncles Vinnie and Billy Morrey who enjoyed modest careers in the game – Billy even played semi-professionally for England.

Says dad Wayne Sr, 'I'm really made up for all my lads – and I hope they can keep it up. They've always wanted to play for Everton, too.'

The family firmly believe they have an ancestor to thank for the fighting spirit which runs in their blood – the soccer star's great-great-grandfather was related to 'Ruby' Bob Fitzsimmons who was crowned the Heavyweight Champion of the World in 1897.

Wayne's uncle Robert Morrey says, 'It's a little-known fact that Wayne is related to Gentleman "Ruby" Bob Fitzsimmons.'

It's a heritage the family are justly proud of – Gentleman 'Ruby' Bob took the middleweight prize title from Jack Dempsey in New Orleans in 1891.

The Cornish-born pugilist – renowned for his good manners – progressed through the ranks and, in 1897, aged 33, he knocked out heavyweight John Corbett with a huge punch during a ferocious bout in Nevada.

Says Robert, brother of Wayne's mum Jeanette, 'We

reckon the warrior spirit is in Wayne's blood – and it's gone to his feet instead of his fists!'

It's no surprise that Robert's yet another of the Rooney clan to have a sporting claim – he lives in Melbourne after emigrating to Australia to play professional football for the Melbourne-Hungaria side.

Wayne himself wasn't immune to the boxing spirit which had inspired his ancestor to greatness. Naturally broad, stocky and thick-set, young Wayne looked every inch a promising boxer and, by the age of seven, was throwing his punches at the local gym, managed by his uncle, Richie Rooney.

The club, run from Croxteth Sports Centre, is located in a green-painted prefab building, frayed around the edges and less than half-a-mile from Wayne's childhood home on Stonebridge Lane.

But, to Wayne and his pals, it was the key to a world of tantalising possibility, a key that might unlock a treasure chest of money which was unlikely otherwise to come their way, even from the weekly lottery which their cash-strapped families cherished fruitless hopes of winning.

Says Wayne, 'Boxing is the second sport in my family. My dad boxed for England and I tried it out as a kid. But I was never a great stylist in the ring – I just got in there and threw plenty of leather! I was OK, though, I did knock a few people over in sparring.

'When I was about 13, I'd spar in my uncle's boxing gym out of season – I was the biggest in my class at school so no one took the mickey out of me. The lad I sparred against was three years older than me but he'd always be a bit dazed when I punched him because, even then, I was a bit heavier than him.

'I used to train in the gym out of season to keep my body strength up but, that year, I was due to go into a boxing match for the amateur schoolboys competition and had to have a medical. I quite liked boxing, but my mum wouldn't let me take the medical. She wanted me to concentrate on my football, so I wasn't allowed to enter the competition.

'I was disappointed, but I believed in myself and I believed in my football and I knew Mum and Dad wanted what was best for me.'

Despite his early promise in the ring, it was Wayne's natural talent as a footballer which was the talk of the town. He may have been just seven years old, but little Wayne Rooney was affectionately regarded as a mouse that roared on the pitch, an acutely shy lad who let his eloquent feet do the talking.

And they didn't just talk – they sang like a choir of angels every time he took to the pitch, housed in a pair of bedraggled trainers, a toe poking through the front, poignant testimony to the financial struggles his parents faced.

His uncle Vinnie, 46, says, 'We all knew Wayne was good at football but most of our family are good at football so we didn't realise the sheer scale of his talent. But his mum and dad were always convinced he was going to be a great player; they'd talk about how brilliantly he was doing every time we all met up for get-togethers at Wayne's gran's house. Wayne was a modest, quiet lad ... it made him blush.'

His sensational skills meant Wayne was already shaping up as a hero to his young schoolmates at Our Lady and St Swithin's Primary School, where his playground prowess was legendary and heralded future glory.

Wayne's playmate – and goalkeeper – Daniel Hinnigan, now 19, recalls, 'We were only young but Wayne's skill blew us away – he always played up with us older lads and was dynamite.

'We all loved football but Wayne lived and breathed it. He would have eaten it if he could. He never talked about anything else; every conversation centred around it.

'He was always practising new tricks, trying them out over and over again until he got them right. He would even skip his lunch at school so he could have that extra ten minutes playing footie during the break.'

That was some sacrifice for the youngster – Wayne relished his food, especially his favourite sausage, beans and chips, which he'd devour before lining up for seconds in the dinner queue if rain had stopped play.

He is remembered as a good pupil, attentive in class and well counselled in the value of faith. His parents, both devout Roman Catholics, were proud as punch when he was chosen to sing in the choir during the school's nativity play.

The moment was immortalised on a video recording, showing Wayne, in shirt and tie, belting out carols with his hands clasped anxiously before him while classmates act out scenes from the Christmas story.

His former headmaster at St Swithin's, Tony McCall,

remembers, 'Wayne was always a very respectful pupil. Whether he was on the football pitch or the stage, he always gave everything his best shot.'

But it was soccer which transformed Wayne from a boy who wouldn't say boo to a goose to a self-assured youngster happy to let his feet do the talking.

Tony, who is still headmaster at the school, said, 'Wayne absolutely loved his football, he shone out even then. It was obvious he could become a great player; he was passionate about the game.

'He came alive on a pitch. He was always very shy but he came out of his shell when he was playing football.'

Football playing was banned at St Swithin's – time and space didn't allow the game to feature on the timetable – but that never stopped the goal-hungry kids.

Makeshift goalposts were created from school jumpers, often resembling moth-eaten rags from the holes caused by such service, as the boys pounded their way to victory during break-time in the playground.

Says Tony, 'Wayne was head and shoulders above the other lads in the playground. He was always a very well-behaved boy but would have been out there all the time if he could have got away with it – he absolutely lived for the game. The kids used to call each other after their heroes – Wayne was always Alan Shearer.

'He was good in his lessons, always tried to give of his best, never caused any problems. His school reports were always good and he was a popular lad, although shy. He was only comfortable with those he knew well.

'He enjoyed his classes but he always shone out in PE, especially on sports day each July. He was so very quick and competitive – whether it was the beanbag race or a straightforward sprint, Wayne nearly always won.

'Both his brothers Graham and John were pupils here and were also exceptional at football. Even back then, I used to have a little daydream where I could see them all one day lining up together for Everton in the Premiership – they were all of them that superb at the game.

'Wayne's a credit to the school and his parents. They really encouraged him; they were dedicated, loved football and were very proud of Wayne.

'These days, all the kids want to be like him and he's set them a good example with his behaviour on and off the pitch. He has done wonders for their esteem, because they know they are at the school Wayne Rooney went to and they're proud of that ... it's made them realise what can be achieved through hard work.

'We talk about him in assembly and say prayers for him. There's no escaping Roomania at this school!'

It was while Wayne was still aged seven that his immense talent first earned him fans, when he played for an Under-12s team from The Western Approaches pub in Storrington Avenue, still a favourite watering hole with his family and known locally as 'The Wezzy'.

It was a bitterly cold day, rain clouds glowering with threat, as excited Wayne frantically flung on his kit, eager to get to the ground where he hoped to play his first game for the team.

He already knew many of the lads, familiar faces from his home territory, some the older brothers of his friends, but still a knot of anxiety twisted in his

CITY OF LIMERICK
35030
PUBLIC LIBRARY

stomach. He was smaller by a foot than most of the players, five years younger and, despite his playground performances, the boy feared he might not match up – he'd never played for an official team before.

As the cold wind whistled around his ears, Wayne sat on the sidelines huddled in an anorak, nervously waiting to come on as a sub. He spoke only when spoken to, sitting cross-legged, shoulders hunched, eyes never leaving the game.

Then, suddenly, his chance came. Mum Jeanette swelled with pride as her lad hurried on to the pitch, giving him a thumbs up for luck, shyly acknowledged with a half-smile from the boy with stardust in his boots.

It's a freeze-frame moment etched on the proud mum's memory for ever. Says Jeanette, 'I'll never, ever forget it. They didn't play football at his primary school and Wayne didn't take part in his first proper game until he was seven, and that was playing for the Under-12s at Storrington. It was his first ever proper game but he came on as a sub – and he scored!'

The sizzling goal left the 'keeper standing and his speechless team-mates rooted to the spot for a split-second before they burst into cheers, mobbing the little lad and almost burying him under the weight of their delight.

It was just a kid's goal, supported by a squall of robust cheers like hundreds of others around the nation that day.

But, unknown to the shivering Sunday morning crowd huddled on the sidelines at the Merseyside ground, they were witnessing history in the making.

Wayne Rooney had arrived – and was about to blaze a scorching trail of victories on his way to becoming an England hero.

Cousin Thomas remembers, 'There was no stopping Wayne. He was playing for the Under-12s team at Storrington when he was seven and was scoring for fun – he got 16 goals in one game!'

Wayne was soon weaving his spell for several other teams, including Pye FC and East Villa – where he was partnered by Thomas for a while – before he was snapped up to bring glory to another pub team, The Copplehouse Colts, in the Walton and Kirkdale Junior League.

But it was his record-breaking performances in the Liverpool Primary Schools league where the seeds of Roomania were first sown. The league had been formed thanks to the dedication of Tim O'Keefe, a deputy headmaster in the south Liverpool district of Chilwell – and the man who nurtured Wayne's burgeoning talents as his coach while he went on a rampage through the league.

The boy was simply a phenomenon, eventually breaking the league's goalscoring record by netting a stunning 72 times in the 1996–97 season – out of a team total of 158 goals.

But it wasn't Rooney's style to swagger. Tim remembers him as an intensely shy boy, an instinctive player whose short-cropped hair, bulldog stare and shark-like instincts then, as now, gave him a menacing edge.

Says Tim, 'Back in the mid-80s we had Steve Redmond who went on to play for Manchester City in our district primary side. He was a defender as a professional, but as an 11-year-old he was a striker. He set a record of 60-plus goals in one season.

'That stood right through until Wayne was playing for us. He was just 10, but he smashed that record out of sight, scoring 72 times in about 33 games.

'We'd had the likes of Steve McManaman and Robbie Fowler go through our teams, and they stood out. Wayne was the same, he had that special something. He was awesome, fearsome at that age. He had quality, he was very strong with controlled aggression and could use either of his feet and his head.

'He didn't take prisoners on the pitch and, sometimes, he could be frustrating because he would go against everything in the coaching manuals. You'd sit there in despair and think, Oh no! He can't do anything from here, nothing. And then you'd suddenly see him put the ball in the net!

'It wasn't so much a case of coaching him as guiding him, because he just went ahead and did his own thing. But Wayne was a good listener. He never said much, just listened and took on board what he was being told.

'He was a level-headed lad, sensible and very quiet and polite, quite shy, although he always looked quite intimidating with his short hair.

'He just let his feet do the talking. I always thought he would end up playing for England – it was obvious he was destined for great things. Put simply, he was a goal machine.'

His team-mates, some now A-level students and others working as trainee plumbers, bank clerks, builders' apprentices and barmen, still relish memories of the soccer sensation's schoolboy skills.

Trainee joiner Paul Leamy, 17, said, 'Wayne was always going to be a star. I remember we played one team and the result was 13–0 and Wayne scored 10 blinding goals! It sticks in my memory as one of the best games of my life.'

And self-employed cabler Jordan Alvis, 18, says, 'Wayne always had power and speed, one hell of a shot. Every game we played was memorable because of him. I still talk about how he destroyed other teams to this day.'

That same year, as Rooney lit up the school pitches, another potent omen of his destiny arrived – his first taste of victory in Europe. The team competed in an international tournament in Holland and lifted the trophy.

But not even in his wildest boyhood fantasies, as he scored against his heroes in feverish dream scenarios in his head, could Wayne have imagined that he'd be walking out as the youngest ever player to put on a shirt for England just seven years later, in a friendly with Australia at Upton Park.

The one thing Wayne loathed about playing for the Liverpool Schools league was pulling on the obligatory red shirt. His family were always true Blue bloods – pledging allegiance to the royal blue of Everton, a club which lived in the gigantic crimson shadow of its cash-rich Merseyside neighbour Liverpool FC, yet inspired unquestionable loyalty in the Rooney household.

That loyalty passed from father to son – dad Wayne Sr

was an Everton fan from the day he first drew breath, and there was never any doubt that his sons would become dedicated devotees, too.

The day Wayne was born at Fazakerley Hospital on 24 October 1985 was the same day his dad bought the lad his first-team shirt.

Just six months later, the tot was wearing the blue-and-white strip for his baptism into the Everton fan club, nestled in the arms of his proud father at Goodison Park – and the boy's name was put down at the club in the hope that he would one day walk out as a mascot.

Says Wayne Sr, 'Like me, Wayne has always been an Evertonian. We're Evertonians through and through. His first match at Goodison Park? He was just six months when I took him!

'Back then, I never really thought about him going all the way, you just don't. We're all so very proud of him.'

The club's pennants waved proudly from the family's three-bedroom council home and, in the windows, posters, stickers and even an Everton car registration plate proclaimed their loyalty.

The Rooney boys' most treasured treat was to spend the weekend watching the ebb and flow of Everton's fortunes – all the lads were season-ticket holders and, together with their cousin Thomas, shouted themselves hoarse under the watchful eye of their uncle Bunter.

Says Thomas, 'We used to go to Everton games with our uncle Bunter when we were kids. It's mad to think Wayne plays for them now – it seems just a moment ago we were spectators yelling from the terraces.'

It is, perhaps, not surprising then that Wayne turned up for a trial with arch-rivals Liverpool stubbornly wearing his prized Everton shirt. He was aged just eight but, already, he had a single ambition – and it wasn't to play in front of a red-shirted crowd on the Kop at Anfield.

His heart was already claimed and marched to the beat on the opposite side of Stanley Park, the stone's throw of no-man's land which separates Goodison Park and Anfield, the hallowed grounds of the two Merseyside rivals.

He told *Evertonian* magazine, 'I actually had a trial for Liverpool. I was playing for Copplehouse Under-9s at the time and, after the game, I was approached by a Liverpool scout who invited me for a trial at the club.

'As a young lad wanting to be a professional footballer, I had to go to Liverpool when I was asked because there was no other club interested in me then.

'I went along but, after going there just once, I got a phone call from an Everton scout. It was the call I had desperately wanted and that was it for me. There was never any doubt in my mind. I gave Liverpool a swerve after that.'

Wayne's white-hot ambition to play for Everton had been founded in the crucible of his true Blue home, but he also felt a fierce desire to reward the sacrifices his mum and dad had made for him. He was acutely aware of how much they'd both given up so their sons might have the chance of a better life.

He'd watched his mum work slavishly long hours and his dad struggle with the trials of injury and unemployment, the grinding trudge to the job centre rarely resulting in work, but neither complaining when it came to scraping together cash for expensive boots or a new team strip so their boys would look as smart as the next.

The sprawling Croxteth estate they called home is by no means the worst in Liverpool, but neither is it the best.

Like many of its kind in Britain, it's a bleak, unprepossessing place, an afterthought plonked on the edge of Liverpool's eastern boundaries and left to lumber towards inevitable decay.

More than half the estate's children qualify for free school dinners and tell-tale signs of wearied neglect point towards the hardships endured behind its doors.

Long-derelict buildings, windows blinded by boarding, are masked by grim, corrugated sheets of steel; empty, vandalised shops are imprisoned behind barbed wire and the ominous buzz of police helicopters is often heard overhead.

Yet there are also signs of hope – new developments begin to mushroom and red-brick terraces with tidy houses speak of the spirited refusal of many to surrender to the acidic corrosion of pride. The Rooney home was one of them.

The boys had few luxuries – and their parents even fewer. Wayne's biggest indulgence was a mountain bike, a Christmas gift for which he'd yearned but had never expected to materialise. The bike was his pride and joy, nurtured with all the care lavished on a baby until he outgrew it at 14.

The family may have owned little, but what they did

have was each other, a close-knit team whose greatest pleasure was a day out at Everton, yelling themselves hoarse at the match as they willed their club to victory, and whose prized possessions were the trophies their sons had won, given pride of place on top of the telly beside scrapbooks bulging with every report noting the boys' successes.

And there was no prouder moment for the Rooney parents than when Wayne got his chance to walk out as a mascot with his beloved team for the derby match that took place on 20 November 1996.

Wayne stood there, ramrod straight, bristling with pride and delight, his eyes seeking out the stand where his thrilled parents cheered wildly.

Later, euphoric Wayne met up with his mum and dad to re-live the highlight of his day – he may have been just nine years old, but he'd chipped Everton and Welsh international goalie Neville Southall from 20 yards in the warm-up.

Photographs of Wayne standing alongside then Everton captain Dave Watson and former Liverpool skipper John Barnes in the Anfield centre circle still have pride of place in his parents' home.

Says Wayne, 'When I walked out as a kid in the Merseyside derby it was hard to imagine I would be playing for Everton one day. I always hoped I would.

'I wanted to play for Everton so badly that I just used to play football in the street all the time, re-living the games pass by pass. All I ever wanted to do was walk out at Goodison Park with our theme tune, *Z-Cars*, playing in the background. I wanted it so much ... As a kid, I used to get shivers down my spine when I heard it and I still do today.'

That same year, Wayne lifted his first youth club trophy – for starring in his own production of his favourite movie musical *Grease* in a youth club competition. He said, 'I loved the film *Grease*, and used to practise the dance moves. When I was about 11 years old, me and four of my mates put on our own production of *Grease* at our youth club – I played Danny, of course! We all knew we were getting leather jackets for Christmas, so our mums gave them to us early to use in our play.

'We practised for months and about 100 people turned up, including all our mums. It was really funny … at the end, we all twirled our jackets around our heads and threw them into the audience – and had to make sure our mums caught them so our jackets wouldn't get dirty before Christmas.

'We won – we got a trophy and about £20 each pocket money. I still love *Grease* and I can still do the moves!'

Typically, Wayne names the greatest football match he has ever watched as one played by Everton. 'I love Everton and the best game I watched as a football fan was against Coventry when Gareth Farrelly scored a goal to keep us up in 1998. It was a 1–1 draw on the last day of the season. I didn't think we'd go down, but I did have my doubts. There was a fantastic atmosphere inside Goodison Park and I'll always remember all the fans on the pitch at the end of the game.

'My first derby match as a player was at Anfield. I got a bit of stick that day and all I could think about on the bench was coming on and scoring so I could wind their fans up. It was a weird feeling when I first played alongside Duncan Ferguson, though, when only a few years back I was standing watching him from the stands.

'I used to idolise him when I was a kid – I've still got a picture I had taken of me when I was a mascot with Duncan – and then, a few years later, I was in the side partnering him and got his autograph.'

Once, when asked at a press conference if he might ever play for Liverpool, his answer was short and swift – 'Who?' he retorted.

But when it came to England, like millions of others, Wayne was blind to the colour of a player's club shirt. He was just 12 years old, crammed with his brothers and cousins around the telly in gran Mavis's front room, when Michael Owen scored his wonder goal against Argentina in the 1998 World Cup.

Says Wayne, 'I remember watching Michael's goal against Argentina. I was 12 and saw the game at my nan's. Afterwards, we all ran out into the garden and recreated it over and over, taking turns in goal – I was quite good there, too!'

As he celebrated the legendary goal, dodging and weaving and belting the ball in his gran's back garden, little did the boy imagine that one day he'd wear the golden crown which had previously been worn by Liverpool's Michael Owen as England's strike king. And that enchanting day would arrive sooner than anybody could predict. On 12 February 2003, he would enthral the nation, becoming the youngest player at 17 years and 111 days to pull on a Three Lions shirt to appear in his first game for England.

As train driver Bob Pendleton, the talent scout who'd brought the boy wonder to Everton, delightedly watched Rooney take his place amongst the greats he, too, was pinching himself to try and believe it wasn't all a dream.

ALAN Shearer ... he'd be my ideal strike partner, because I used to watch him as a kid and I tried to model myself around HIM.

2

TRUE BLUE

THE DAY DAWNED crisp and clear, a chill nip of winter already in the air. Train driver Bob Pendleton cupped his mug of tea, warming his hands, as he prepared for his usual Sunday ritual.

Watching schoolboys play soccer could be a thankless task, as Bob knew only too well. Talent scouting for his beloved club Everton was his sideline and an unquenchable passion but, when frost lay on the ground and rain threatened, it took an iron will to drag himself from the warmth of home and along to the muddy pitches.

Bob was a man who could spot raw talent a mile off. He'd watched hundreds of matches in his lifetime, mostly unmemorable, but every boy a hero to his parents as he marched off the pitch to be consoled or congratulated.

It had been a long time, too long, since Bob had seen

a lad with the kind of gift who could make the hair on your head stand on end.

He'd seen talent for sure, boys who could score good goals, dodge and weave, use their heads or make good passes. Brilliance, though, had passed them by and he was beginning to wonder if he'd ever experience again the spine-tingling thrill of witnessing the unmistakable hallmark of a genuine star in the making.

But today would be different. Today, Bob would discover his star, a boy blessed with such luminary skill that he set the pitch ablaze.

Wayne was just nine years old playing for Copplehouse Under-10s in the Walton and Kirkdale Junior Football League, but destiny was standing on the sidelines, huddled in an anorak, and the boy's life was about to change for ever.

Proud Bob, now 64, recalls, 'You could tell he was special straight away. When you see someone special, you just know, you feel your hair rising.'

It was a feeling only too familiar to the managers of the tiny Copplehouse Colts team, retired window cleaner Nev Davies and delivery driver John McKeown.

They'd taken a call from the pub team at The Wezzy in 1994, who explained they were an Under-12s side but had a boy playing for them, just nine years old, who was a scoring sensation. Would they like to take a look? Would they!

The duo shot over to the Rooney home in Croxteth the next evening.

Says McKeown, 41, 'We headed over to the Rooney

place and Wayne was outside, kicking a ball around in the street.

'We spoke to his mum and arranged to take a look at him the next day. Well, we had become quite blasé about meeting parents, giving trials, saying "yes" or "no" to young kids.

'This time, we saw Wayne unleash a stunning overhead kick; he looked years ahead of anyone we had ever seen and we literally drove at 70mph back to his house to complete the signing.

'He was phenomenal. All he ever wanted to do was score and he was miles better than anyone else.'

And Nev, 40, whose son Ryan used to set up young Rooney's goals from midfield, remembers predicting the fledgling star's rise to greatness. He says, 'From the off, I said he would be better than Michael Owen or Robbie Fowler. He always had big, strong thighs and was more in the Alan Shearer mould, riding the tackles and playing with a fantastic awareness.

'Wayne was unbelievable, always playing in the team a year above. We had him for 18 months. Needless to say, he scored on his début and once hit 12 in a 14-goal onslaught.

'In the first season, he helped us to an Under-10s cup triumph and then we joined Liverpool's top league, the Walton and Kirkdale. He was fantastic there, too. He was so good, he never practised with us. He was a throwback to when lads learned their craft in the street.

'But we picked him up in the minibus on Saturday morning, he'd listen to our instructions and off he would go. He was a shy lad but very attentive. His dad, very often with his mum, was always there encouraging. He never got on Wayne's back.

'After 40 or so goals in the second season, John and I turned down the chance of a bet that Wayne would become the youngest kid to play for Everton and then the youngest kid to play for England.

'Joe Royle pipped him to the Everton part but, after eclipsing Michael Owen as the Premiership's youngest scorer, the England bit, also held by Owen, was too good to miss!'

It was Nev who had tipped off scout Pendleton about the boy. Now, Bob stood rooted to the spot, transfixed by the sublime scene unfolding hypnotically before his eyes. It was a once-in-a-lifetime moment, a moment of unadulterated magic.

Says Bob, 'From the word go, the things Wayne could do with the ball, the goals he could score, he was a natural. Even then, he was so comfortable on the ball, he was just one of them born players ... amazing.'

Within minutes, buzzing with excitement, Bob hastily sought out team manager John.

He says, 'I approached their manager John and asked him, "What's the name of the little fellow?" He looked at me and groaned, "Oh, Bobby," he said, "we've only just signed him. Leave him alone." I stared at him and said, "Leave him alone? You must be joking!"

'Wayne was strong and dedicated and couldn't stop scoring goals. The manager pointed out his mum and dad, big Wayne and Jeanette, over on the other side of the pitch.

'I went over and introduced myself and said I'd like to

take the young man into Bellefield for a trial at the Everton Academy. The look on their faces, because they were Evertonians, said it all. I knew I was on to a winner.'

The trouble was, arch-rivals Liverpool had got there first. The club's scouts had seen him performing in a Saturday league in the Bootle area and young Rooney had already been for a training session.

Explains Nev, 'A Liverpool scout had approached me and suggested Wayne had a trial. The Rooneys have always been true Blue, but they agreed I should take him along to Melwood because I was a Liverpool fan.

'It was strange … he played well and scored several times in seven-a-side but the coaches were stand-offish and didn't make a fuss of him. Wayne wasn't too disappointed. Next, I told Bob about him. He came to see him and his eyes immediately lit up.

'This time John, because he supports Everton, went with Wayne and his mum to the Everton Academy, where his performance was noted straight away. It was the end of the 1995/96 season and Wayne never played for Copplehouse again.'

Bob takes up the story, recalling in the *Guardian*, 'On the Thursday, I went over and had a little chat with Ray Hall, the director of Everton's Academy and said, "I'm bringing the little fellow in." Wayne had been for a training session with Liverpool but he only ever wanted to do one thing and that was play for Everton.

'It doesn't matter what Liverpool would have said to him, he wouldn't have gone there. His dad, Wayne Sr, also said he wasn't going anywhere else. He was also adamant he wasn't going to end up with Liverpool.

'Wayne has set the city on fire. He was born to score goals. It's a real Roy of the Rovers story. I've been asked if I think I'll ever find another Rooney and the answer is always the same – "Jesus, no!"'

'A good friend said to me, "You only find one of them in your lifetime, so sit back and enjoy the ride Wayne is going to give you," and I am enjoying it. It's emotional at times, but I'm sure Wayne's going through the same!'

Lifelong Everton fan Rob 'Macca' McCarthy, 31, also remembers the first time he saw Wayne Rooney at Everton's training ground, and began to see for himself that the rumours about a new wonderkid could actually be true.

'I am going back now to nearly three-and-a-half years ago, and everybody was talking about a lad who had started training at Bellefield, saying he was going to be the next Gazza.

'I went down to Croxteth one Sunday to watch him playing for a pub team, it was The Western Approaches (The Wezzy), and the other players in the team were all in their mid-twenties and looked the sort that loved a good punch-up, most of them had flattened noses and close cropped hair. The opposition team were from Speke in south Liverpool and they, too, looked just like the "broken-nose brigade".

'When I first set eyes on Wayne, I thought that he was going to get eaten alive by the opposition players who would not have looked out of place as club doormen. But my fears were unfounded ... I couldn't believe what I was seeing as Wayne left his prey for dead. As he raced forward with the ball, several of the opposing players would try to kick lumps out of him but he danced and weaved his way through them.

'I honestly thought that he was going to get hurt by these men but he gave as good as he got, though – I heard a couple of the opposing players squeal and groan as they went down under one of Wayne's bone-crunching tackles.

'This was a schoolboy playing and holding his own against grown men who liked nothing better than intimidating and giving their opponents harsh tackles. Well, it was they who received a lesson … nothing that they could do had any effect on young Wayne – he was not in the slightest bit afraid of them. He was fearless.

'Wayne went on to score two goals and had a hand in the third goal; his team ended up winning 3–1.

'I still wonder to this day if the opposing players knew that he was only a schoolboy, as they would kick him up in the air and watch as he got back up and come back for more.

'I went to watch him on a number of occasions after that; he had the aggression of Graham Souness and the skills of Diego Maradona and Kenny Dalglish all rolled into one.

'The touchline would be jam-packed with people who had come just to see Wayne play, even arthritic pensioners who would sit in wheelchairs with their check blankets over the laps, the only time they would bother to venture outdoors in the week – and this in the dead of winter.

'That's the effect Wayne had on people. These same pensioners were comparing him to the great Duncan

Edwards, one of the Busby Babes who perished in the Munich air disaster in 1958, these comparisons being made by old men who had seen Duncan Edwards play.

'They would also compare him to Billy Liddle, a Liverpool footballing legend from many years ago and they were making these comparisons about a lad who was still in school. He was just phenomenal.'

Everton's Academy director Ray Hall has worked on the club's youth development for 12 years and coaxed and cajoled a galaxy of future stars through their paces. But even he was gripped by an instantaneous thrill when he first witnessed Rooney in action. He signed the boy after just one training session.

'I didn't even need that as proof,' he says. 'When you get an experienced scout sitting there quivering while you're talking to the lad, you know he's a special talent,' he told the *Guardian*. 'We had started hearing a lot about this lad, even when he was an Under-9 player. When Bob brought him in, he was trembling, his tea was spilling all over the place because he was so excited.'

Ray knew he had a rare talent on his hands. But it wasn't until he took the lad with an Under-11 team to play at Manchester United's training ground that he recognised his signing was bursting with magic. Wayne was just ten years old but delivered a performance so stunning it hushed the awed crowd into silence.

Ray remembers, 'The first time I realised how special he could be was when I took an Under-11 team to play at Man U's training ground. It was eight-a-side on small pitches with small goals. There were hundreds of

Top: Wayne with mum Jeanette.

Bottom: A jubilant Wayne leaps to acknowledge the fans as Everton beat Newcastle United 2–1 in April 2003.

England's hero is ready to take on Switzerland.

In 1994, Wayne, far left, won the Copplehouse Player of the Year trophy. His t-shirt says 'Everton Dogs of War'.

Top: Honing that formidable kick, Wayne at Copplehouse in 1994.

Bottom: As an 11-year-old in 1996, Wayne was the proud mascot for Everton before the Liverpool Derby. With him is legendary Everton captain Dave Watson, far left.

Top: Wayne, middle row, second from left, with the rest of the boys at Copplehouse.

Bottom: In Switzerland for a tournament with Everton, Wayne lines up far right. Third from right is Anthony Gerrard, cousin of Liverpool's Steven Gerrard.

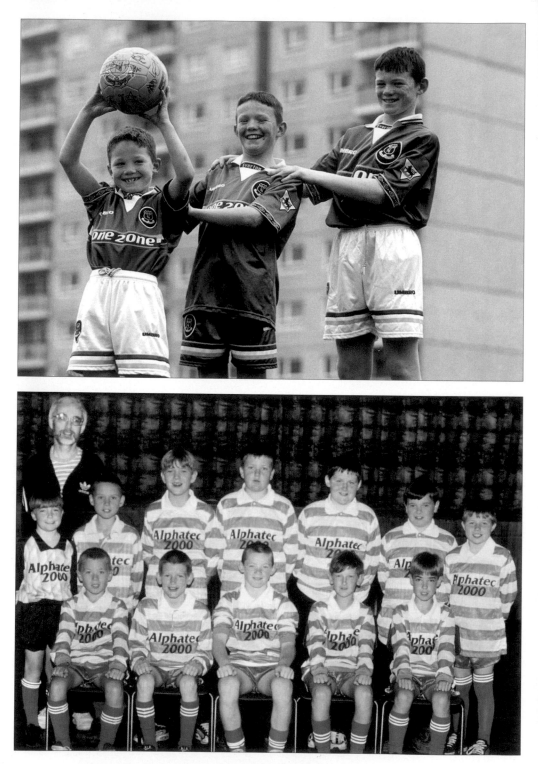

Top: The brothers Rooney – John, Graham and Wayne – have all signed up with Everton. Who else?

Bottom: Wayne at 11, seated centre, with the St Swithins Primary School team and their headmaster.

Top: Wayne Rooney, Copplehouse manager John McKeown and Graham Rooney after signing for Everton in 1994. When McKeown first watched Wayne at work, he said, 'He looked years ahead of anyone we had ever seen.'

Bottom: Everton's Duncan Ferguson with the Rooneys: Wayne said, 'I used to idolise him when I was a kid and then, a few years later, I was in the side partnering him and got his autograph.'

Top: Number 18, part one: Wayne gets ready to tuck into a slice of 18th birthday cake with Harry Layden at the Alder Hey Hospital.

Bottom: Number 18, part two: flanked by Everton manager David Moyes and chairman Bill Kenwright, Wayne celebrates signing a new contract with the club in January 2003.

people there. All the parents were on one side of the pitch, the coaches on the other as the match started.

'Someone played a ball over. The ball was crossed but it went behind Wayne. Instead of controlling it or trying to head it, he executed a scissor-kick from 10 to 15 yards out and the ball flew straight into the top corner of the net.

'There was total silence around the ground ... you could have heard a pin drop. Out of nowhere, I heard one parent, Wayne's dad I think, start to clap. Then it became a slow ripple of applause and, within a few seconds, everyone was clapping him like thunder, even the United parents were applauding. It was unforgettable.'

The boy wonder later went on to score a record-breaking 99 goals for the Academy's Under-10s in one season.

Hall's department is one of the biggest at Everton because producing their own home-grown talent is crucial for the cash-strapped club. He says, 'There is something about this area, because it has always produced outstanding talent, not only for us but also Liverpool and Tranmere Rovers. It must be in the genes.

'Francis Jeffers came here aged nine and was in the first team as a teenager. Wayne was the same age when he arrived. They are both local lads; they went to the same junior and secondary schools and they made their full England débuts together against Australia.

'You can never be sure how far a young boy will progress in football but Franny and Wayne were always at the top of their age groups for ability and potential.

'I remember the first time I saw Franny and it was

obvious he was an intelligent and gifted lad. He scores most of his goals inside the penalty area but that is a knack in itself. With Wayne, the goals can come from anywhere because he is physically the stronger of the pair. I am sure neither of them will rest on their laurels – you get an appetite for success in this game.

'In recent years, we have produced four England internationals in Jeffers, Rooney, Michael Ball and Gavin McCann, plus Richard Dunne for the Republic of Ireland. And five of the ten youngest goalscorers in the Premiership came from here – Jeffers and Rooney again, plus Ball, Michael Branch and Danny Cadamarteri. Since our Academy was established in 1995, 17 players have gone on to play for the first team.

'Wayne has done brilliantly. Every challenge he has been faced with he has met and raised the bar. Nothing seems to faze him. He has always played over his own age which is probably why he's so comfortable with the England squad. He's the youngest but he's used to that. He's no different from the kid at school who is a gifted mathematician and is moved up classes to be with kids of his own ability.'

The Everton Academy was truly a family affair for the Rooneys – back in 1998, Wayne and his brothers Graham and John all played for the club's youth teams. John remains but Graham has left to concentrate on the family's second love – boxing.

Says Ray, 'It was the first time in history that we had three brothers all playing here at the same time, and all talented.'

As with all kids at the Academy, Wayne was taken

under the wing of a welfare officer from the moment he was signed up. It's the officer's job to keep an eagle eye on the boys' development, to ensure they're not under too much pressure or unhealthily obsessed by performance. Gently, over time, the youngsters are schooled in the pitfalls of fame, how to behave in a fashion which credits the game and how to handle attention from the public and media.

Ray says, 'There are five bubbles surrounding a player. Every player has to cope with their own rate of technical development, physical growth, physiological progress and mental development. We have technical coaches and fitness coaches and a medical department and sports scientists, but by far the biggest bubble is their social and emotional development. At Goodison Park, players are presented with a code of conduct and every year they are reminded that they have a duty to behave well.

'If we've done anything for Wayne, we've improved his social life and skills. He was a timid boy when he came here but we give the players life-skills training on how to manage the media and all that goes with the glitz.'

It wasn't just Wayne's scintillating skill which stood out but also his mental strength. He was a shy, taciturn boy who kept his thoughts to himself.

But already he was developing the focused discipline which would catapult him on to the world stage with lightning speed. The practice pitches used by the Academy were a mile away from De La Salle, the Catholic secondary school where Rooney was a pupil.

Yet he was always the first to arrive, leaping on to his mountain bike the second the school bell rang at 3.30pm and pedalling as fast as his legs could carry him to the patchily turfed theatre of his dreams. There, alone, he recreated his favourite goals, zig-zagging across the pitch and shooting over and over, a vivid commentary running in his head, until training started at 5.00pm.

Says Hall, 'Wayne never missed a session, never gave us a moment's problem, and had this terrific, supportive family that let us get on with the job.'

His former PE teacher at De La Salle, Joe Hennighan, also remembers Rooney's dedication. 'Wayne was not particularly academic – young lads love sport and, if you live in this city, there is only one sport they are going to play, and that is football.

'Once Wayne started playing, it was obvious he was going to go far. He was a really good competitor and always physically very able.'

Rooney, always a stocky lad, suddenly shot up in size when he was 13, towering over the other boys in his class. Says Joe, 'Wayne was the biggest lad in his class and his size was the thing you always noticed first. I've always said you've got to be strong to get a muffin in the dinner queue at De La Salle!'

Briefly, Wayne's football form suffered as his body adapted and he struggled to master his limbs, but his unerring discipline never wavered. His worried parents would often call the Academy, concerned that their son had not returned home and Wayne, more often than not, would be found pounding the treadmill at the specially equipped gym.

CITY OF LIMERICK PUBLIC LIBRARY

Sometimes, though, as with any boy, Wayne's halo slipped. He would naughtily sneak off to the local bookie's with a pal to play on the fruit machines – his height made him appear older than his years – or off to his uncle Richie's boxing gym for a bout of body-building sparring with his cousin in Croxteth.

His fuming mum Jeanette would tear him off a strip when the lad eventually tipped up at home, attempting to look a picture of innocence but resignedly knowing, as with all mums, that she had eyes in the back of her head and beyond.

Today, at 5ft 10in, Wayne's an average height for a player but his bulk – he's 12st 4lb – and his wide-shouldered boxer's physique make him an unstoppable bulldozer on the pitch. That, and Wayne's cleanness of shot, have invited comparisons with former England skipper Alan Shearer. And that's music to Wayne's ears.

As a youngster, he avidly studied his hero until details of the superstar's legendary goalgetting were etched into his memory, later taking to the street for an action replay with himself in the shoes of Shearer.

'He'd be my ideal strike partner,' Wayne told the official Everton website, 'because I used to watch him as a kid and I tried to model myself around him.'

Wayne's star was soon fixed in the firmament at the Everton Academy as he blazed through the ranks like a comet, a trail of glittering milestones left in ashes as he flashed by. At Under-12 level, he played for the Under-13s; at Under-15 he played for the Under-17s and even the Under-19s. By 16, he was playing with the professionals.

One man remembers only too well the 14-year-old Rooney – Walter Smith, then Everton manager, was sitting in his office at the training ground, tackling paperwork, when he chanced to look up.

Outside on the pitch, an Under-17 game was in full flow. Suddenly, Smith felt he'd been struck by a bolt of lightning as a bulky, shaven-haired lad let rip a bullet-like shot from the 45-yard line.

He says, 'I just took a couple of minutes to have a look at the game going on outside. I saw this kid run a yard into the opposition half and then unleash this magnificent shot. I don't think it went in, but I remember thinking to myself, My God, who *is* that?

It was something I had only ever seen Pele and David Beckham try. Not many would try that, never mind a youngster.

'When I asked who he was, our youth team coach Colin Harvey told me and then said, "By the way boss, he's only 14!" I was amazed.'

Smith, talking in the *People*, added, 'When Wayne was only 14, Colin would use him as a sub for the Under-17s and when he was 15 he was playing in the Under-18 and Under-19 teams. And he would come on and score nearly every time. We realised we had a youngster who was very special.

'Going into the training ground on a Saturday morning before first-team games at Goodison, I'd watch Wayne playing against much older boys, scoring goals from every angle. It was incredible.'

Rooney was already scoring the kind of spectacular goals usually confined to the peak of the Premiership.

To his joy, the devoted Toffeeman got his chance to stuff Liverpool in the first Under-19s Merseyside derby of the 2001 season.

Hundreds of fans had converged on Everton's training ground, Bellefield, and those in the red shirts of Liverpool were smugly anticipating victory, their team sitting on a 2–1 lead with just 15 minutes until the final whistle.

Rooney watched anxiously from the bench, every fibre of his body tense, fervently hoping he'd get the chance to help the team grab victory from the drooling red jaws of defeat. Then, as Liverpool got ready to take a corner, Everton brought on the deadliest weapon from their schoolboy arsenal. Rooney strolled on to the pitch and scored the equaliser from a corner taken by David Carney. With nail-biting minutes to spare, Rooney triumphed again as he struck a supernova volley from the edge of the penalty area which exploded into the Liverpool net.

It was the last kick of the game and it instantly wiped out the smiles on the Reds' faces. The result was 3–2 to Everton ... and Roomania was born. And he was still only 16.

The dismay of the Liverpool fans hung heavy in the air and, later that week, the club made a raid for Rooney, hoping to prise him away from Goodison Park.

But the boy stayed resolutely where he was, pledging his future to the Everton Academy. Such was the club's relieved glee, it triumphantly paraded Rooney in front of 38,615 fans during the half-time interval of a Premiership game against Derby County on 15 December.

The lad was cheered to the rafters but some of the

Toffees' fans felt torn, unable to accept a boy barely out of short trousers being subjected to such high-profile adulation so soon, and voicing their unease on fanzine websites. Even so, they couldn't help but gloat ...

Just months later, that same unease would be heard from players, managers and commentators alike when England boss Sven-Göran Eriksson knighted Rooney with the honour of becoming the squad's youngest ever player.

But Rooney was surrounded by a ring of steel, an armour-plated team of family, friends and advisers who had vowed to protect him, and did. What's more, the lad had his head screwed on. He'd trained for the moment from the age of nine, becoming a finely honed goal machine through hours and hours of relentless practice. He'd dreamed of this moment all his short life, breathed football, slept football, played football, talked football, learned football. No worries.

But before his chance came on the international stage, Rooney had a single aim – to lift the Football Association Youth Cup with Everton.

The mesmeric striker was rarely troubled on his successful mission, ramming home thunderbolt goals in almost every match. Manchester City were among the first to fall victim to the sharp end of Rooney's boot, both in the league and the Cup tussle.

Like an express train, Rooney appeared unstoppable, coming on as a sub in the league game and slamming home a winning cannonball strike within five minutes of stepping on to the pitch, and then scoring twice in the 4–2 Youth Cup conquest.

West Bromwich fared no better, falling victim to the

dazzling skills of their young opponent as he bobbed and weaved past players as if they were lead-footed and rocketed home two stunning goals, lobbing the 'keeper from 20 yards for his crushing finale.

Nottingham Forest met the same fate in the quarter-finals, Rooney repeating the amazing scissor-kick which had earned him his place at Everton – and earned his team a goal against their Youth Cup rivals. Later, he set up a goal for defender David Carney, who buried the winner in the 2–1 triumph.

But it was the match against Tottenham Hotspur at White Hart Lane which would ignite the unprecedented interest in Rooney's talent ... and the steady flow of fruitless bids for his services.

Spurs manager Glenn Hoddle was gobsmacked by the boy's soul-tingling performance – and dispirited to discover he wasn't for sale. The reason was obvious – Rooney had already set up a 3-1 lead on aggregate for the Everton team when, in the thirty-seventh minute, he unleashed a goal so spectacular the only appropriate response was to gawp in wonder – and that included Hoddle.

Everton had been given a free kick 30 yards from goal and Rooney, never one to miss an opportunity, reckoned he might just have a go.

He sent the disappointing shot curling straight into the Spurs wall but, as the ball ricocheted off a defender and ballooned up into the air, Rooney ghosted beneath the arc of the ball, took it on his chest and, before it had chance to touch the ground, sent it crashing into the top corner with his left foot.

The *Roon of the Rovers* story didn't end there – he went on to score eight in his campaign, one short of the record shared by Liverpool's Michael Owen and Arsenal's Jeremie Alladiere, and had 25 goal notches on his bedpost by the end of the season.

But the best was yet to come.

I'M more scared of my mum than I am of Sven-Göran Eriksson! She's always ready to hand me a slap if I get out of LINE.

3

PLAYING AT HOME

WHEN ROONEY MADE his competitive début for England, thrown into the cauldron of a European Championship tie against Turkey at Sunderland's Stadium of Light, there were two fans he wanted to please more than any others – his mum and dad.

The couple, Jeanette and Wayne Sr, were fiercely proud of their three boys and were determined that they shouldn't go without.

Given the meagre income Jeanette and Wayne Sr managed to pull in each week, it meant the family lived on a tight budget, working together to make the best use of their money. Like others on the estate in Croxteth, the boys often wore hand-me-down clothes; Jeanette's weekly treat was a game of bingo, and Wayne Sr's was a pint or two down The Wezzy or a trip to nearby Aintree racecourse, where he sometimes took his excited lads to watch the horses thundering home.

The couple kept laying hens in their garden for fresh eggs, and there was also Wayne Sr's pigeon loft, his prized birds having been trained to return home in races against competitors, sometimes being released on day trips to the nearby Welsh mountains or from as far as the Lake District, from where they'd find the quickest route back to Stonebridge Lane.

The boys were encouraged to take part in sport, as a way of keeping them off the streets and to instil in them discipline, and in the silent hope that they might excel.

When Wayne Jr was born at Liverpool's Fazakerley Hospital, the family was convinced his future lay in the ring, his dad even boasting, 'Look, we've got a prize fighter!'

Wayne's aunt Janet, 45, who was present at his birth, says, 'When Wayne was born, all anybody could talk about were these massive hands he'd been blessed with. He was a difficult birth because he was just so big. And he was always a real cutie, all huge eyes and big ears.

'I remember his dad beaming from ear to ear and all the men of the family were convinced that he was to make a fine, professional boxer. He certainly had the body for it, he was massive. Wayne has always been an early developer, so he towered over most of his cousins and had a fine physique.

'But it was obvious from when he was two that football would be his sport – he had a ball constantly stuck to his feet ... he used to bring a ball with him even when he came for his tea. And even though his uncle was mad keen on getting him into boxing, it was the football which lay closest to his heart.

'There was no pressure from the family to choose either one, we just wanted him to be happy and we're all delighted he focused on footie now.'

Jimmy Albertina still coaches Wayne's younger brother Graham at the Rotunda Boxing Club in nearby Kirkdale, where the lad has already made a name for himself. He remembers, 'Wayne only boxed for about a year and it was always a second sport to him. He was a good little fighter and could have had real potential if he had stuck at it. His family didn't have enough cash for the equipment but there was plenty here that he could borrow. But he belongs on the football pitch and not in the ring.

'Boxing really helps improve balance, though, so I like to think that my training helped some way to making Wayne the footballer he is today.'

Wayne's mum had a stern reputation as a no-nonsense woman, one who would brook no argument from the teenagers who lined up in the dinner queue while she was on duty at the all-boys De La Salle School.

It's a job she keeps to this day, insisting she'd be bored if she had to give it up and even securing permission from Liverpool's Lord Mayor to take time off work to see her son play at Euro 2004.

Wayne's former agent Peter McIntosh remembers, 'In the day, Jeanette would work as a dinner lady and then go and do another job. I remember she did so many hours she often didn't have time to go and watch Wayne play for Everton. She was the breadwinner because Wayne's dad was out of work.

'She knew that everything relied on her. Wayne never

wanted for anything, whether it was training shoes or money for going out. Both of Wayne's parents went without so they could do the best for their sons.'

Jeanette ruled her sons with a rod of iron, determined to keep them on the straight and narrow but always there as the first line of defence if anybody dared criticise her boys. Says Wayne, 'I'm more scared of my mum than I am of Sven-Göran Eriksson! She's always ready to hand me a slap if I get out of line.'

But she was also ready to hand out a piece of her mind if she felt her lads were being treated unfairly. She took a dim view when her youngest son John was ditched from the Everton Academy for being overweight, marching down to the training ground to have it out with the coaches. Fuming Jeanette insisted John had the potential to be every bit as good as Wayne and, within days, John was reinstated, testament to Jeanette's forceful belief in justice.

Says Peter McIntosh, 'Jeanette just knows what is best for her lads and she believes in them. She is what you might call a strong character. She isn't one of these women who doesn't know anything about football. She knew about the offside rule, she knew when a player was playing well or badly. She never criticised Wayne. She was always upbeat and she told him he was doing well.

'She was a very strong woman, a lot like Wayne in many ways. She was a quiet, independent type who just got on with her life and her sons were at the centre of it.'

Jeanette's reputation as a tough cookie even travelled as far as the England squad. When once asked before a match what time kick-off was, Steven Gerrard joked, 'When Wayne's mum gets here!'

Tony Melia, who lived next door to the Rooneys throughout Wayne's childhood, has first-hand knowledge of the influence Jeanette has had over her son's career, and in the shaping of his character. He believes it's Wayne's long-suffering mum who should get the credit for raising one of England's brightest talents.

He says, 'Jeanette gave up a lot to get Wayne where he is today and to support his dream of being a footballer. Wayne Sr was out of work for a long time when the boys were young and Jeanette worked her fingers to the bone to support the family. She is a formidable woman and she definitely wears the trousers in that household. She is fearless and, if Wayne or his brothers ever stepped out of line, she would certainly let them know who was boss. There were times when you could hear her shouting through the walls and she did not stand for any messing as far as the kids were concerned.

'She's so proud of what Wayne has achieved and I think part of that pride is because she knows she helped him get there in some way. His mum and dad are the biggest influences on his life and I would say his mum is definitely the most influential.'

Like most riled women, Jeanette had the capacity to make grown men quake in their boots when it came to protecting her brood, but she's a softie at heart. She wept when Wayne scored his first Premiership goal; she wept when he first pulled on a Three Lions shirt and she wept when he scored his first goal for England.

And so did his overwhelmed dad. He was pictured

wiping a tear from his eye as Wayne blew the socks off everyone at Euro 2004, even jubilantly punching the air and performing a spontaneous little jig in front of the delirious crowds chanting his son's name.

Says Jeanette, 'Wayne's just like his dad, they're like two peas in a pod. We're all really excited about seeing all the games Wayne plays in, no matter where. I've always been proud of him – even as a lad, he played for a team called Pye FC and he won his first Golden Boot with them after scoring the most goals in the BT Challenge Cup competition. I've still got that trophy. I'm the proudest mum in the world.

'I remember when he scored his first Premiership goal against Arsenal, we celebrated for ages, I almost lost my voice. But my son is a level-headed lad, he will be able to keep his feet on the ground.'

His dad Wayne Sr was just as thrilled and, inevitably, names his finest moment as the day Wayne first scored for his club in the Premiership.

He says, 'It was the proudest moment of my life. I'll never forget it, I can recall every second of it even now. To see my son score for my team was out of this world. I'm sure it's the first of many goals – and I hope I see them all.'

Wayne's dad likes to joke now that his son's future was already written in the stars when he was born – the Toffees were top of Division One at the time of his birth and the young star was conceived during an 18-match unbeaten run to the title!

Both Wayne's parents are anxious that he should remain close to his roots, protected by his family and shielded from the explosive pressure-cooker of fame. They are delighted by the adulation surrounding their son, but are determined that it should be remembered where he has come from, that he is proud of his heritage and, as yet, has much to learn.

It led his dad to fire off a volley of his own when his son was heavily criticised after he accepted the BBC Young Sports Personality of the Year Award in 2002, chewing gum and with his tie loosened. The young Rooney was accused of behaving in an uncouth fashion but his dad fumed, 'We are very proud of Wayne. Winning the award is a massive achievement for our Wayne and shows how far he has come in such a little time. He is only a young lad and people need to remember that.

'My son is fantastic, he plays his heart out. It is what he does on the pitch that matters and not if he is chewing gum, I don't care what anyone says. We are happy for him, Wayne really deserved that award and that's all there is to it.'

The couple had spent their whole lives on the Croxteth estate where they had raised their children, surrounded by their extended family. They hoped to remain there, anxious to keep their lives on a familiar path, close to their friends and the places they had known all their lives.

Neither wanted to be captured in the bubble of fame surrounding their son, happy to leave their lives unaltered as an example to their boy and as a steadying influence on the heady glamour of his glittering career.

But they had no choice. Wayne's mum was besieged by

fans when she attended a function at Liverpool's Adelphi Hotel, signing autographs simply 'Wayne's mum'.

Fans and reporters knocked at the door of their home but, worse, the family became plagued by vandals. Thugs slashed the tyres on the family's new Ford Galaxy people carrier twice in one week and their home was later attacked with a paintball gun.

Three pellets filled with green paint were fired at the terraced home, one hitting the brickwork and two the upper window where an Everton pennant fluttered in the wind.

A fourth pellet hit the family car. The culprits were suspected to be rival Liverpool fans but Wayne's dad was reluctant to go to the police. He said at the time, 'We don't know why people are doing it. I think maybe they are jealous. We are not going to report it to the police because there is nothing we can do.'

Wayne was still living at home with his parents at the time and insisted on buying them a £470,000 house in nearby West Derby, first offering to send them on holiday while their new home was decorated.

True to her down-to-earth form, Jeanette asked for a £250 three-day break to Butlin's holiday camp in Minehead, Somerset, for the family, a treat which had to be cancelled at the last minute after details were leaked to the press.

The couple's new home, boasting en-suite bathrooms, balconied bedrooms, bay windows and a double garage, is in Sandfield Park, a ten-minute drive from Croxteth and surrounded by top-of-the-range security.

But it was a wrench for the couple to leave behind the

home where their happy memories remained – so Wayne gave his dad the £18,630 to buy it as an investment property and keep it in the family, taking advantage of a 60 per cent discount under the council's right-to-buy scheme.

He employed his uncle Eugene, a builder, to convert the terraced home, splashing out £10,000 on a new roof, double glazing and a conservatory. It proved a lure for trophy-hunters, who rooted through the skip outside and even took the family's old loo seat!

Wayne also moved home, upping sticks with his fiancée Coleen McLoughlin to exclusive Formby, snapping up the £900,000 mansion where they live in luxury today.

But he hasn't forgotten the family he left behind. His parents' former council house is intended as a new home for his unemployed cousin Lisa, 27, a single mum struggling to bring up her two children Rory, four, and Samuel, two, in a grim, mouse-infested house on the Croxteth estate.

She says, 'What Wayne is doing for me is typical of him ... he's always been really kind and he's close to all the family. The house has had £10,000 spent on it and looks like a palace now. I'm dead grateful, it means so much to me and the kids.

'Our Wayne isn't the kind to have his head turned by fancy people or things. He's always been one of the family and that's the way he'll stay. He's ever so generous but he'd never boast about anything like that, he's dead modest. He loves his family more than anything.'

His aunts, uncles and cousins couldn't agree more.

Aunt Janet Gildea, his mum's sister, said at her three-bed semi on the Croxteth estate, 'No matter how famous Wayne becomes, I know he'll still be coming round for his tea. He's a very down-to-earth lad and has a sensible head on his shoulders. We all just treat him as good old Wayne at family get-togethers – he gets no superstar treatment and he doesn't want any. He comes to visit at least once a week and just sits down and chats with a can of Coke like the rest of the kids.'

Her daughter, Wayne's cousin, Toni, 21, often accompanied the star to matches when he was a youngster, frequently getting mistaken for his girlfriend. She says, 'We used to watch the matches with Wayne's dad at first. But, as we got older and wanted more independence, we started going on our own, getting the bus into town and getting chips before kick-off. Wayne was aged about 14 at that time, but he was already a famous face at Goodison. He had signed on the books for the Youth Academy, was playing regularly and scoring goals. So all the fans on the terraces knew who he was and there was already talk that he was going to be something special.

'People used to tease him about me, asking whether I was his sweetheart. Most fans would want to chat to Wayne and start asking us questions about where we went on dates, but he just got really embarrassed by it. Wayne wasn't interested in girls back then, all he could talk about was football and how Everton played.

'I was a bit of a tomboy back then, so I got on with my male cousins the best. Wayne only started taking his eye off the football to look at girls when he was nearly 16. I used to tease him a little that girls would never be interested in him if he spent all his time playing football – but look at him now!

'We were great mates and had our own little secrets and we still are; there's nothing Wayne loves better than to just come round to our house and have a chat about things happening in our lives. He's interested in the family, in normal things, but he likes to treat us, too. He has bought season tickets for my uncle, granddad, my cousin and me in the main stand. Wayne has always been close to the family and wants us to share in his success.'

His nan Patricia, 73, who also lives on the Croxteth estate, is proud as punch of her grandson, one of 37 grandchildren. She's recently been provided with a pacemaker, and is under strict instructions not to jump or punch the air when her grandson scores. But it doesn't stop Patricia and her husband William sharing in the joy of Wayne's success.

She says, 'We're all so proud of Wayne. I'm the proudest gran in England and my husband Billy feels the same way. We've decorated our house with pictures of Wayne, we even have one in the window, and everyone round Croxteth knows who I am.

'I get so excited when I watch him play, I can't look at the telly. So I watch the match in bed and, when he's going for goal, I put my hand over my eyes.

'I remember when he did his cartwheel at Euro 2004, it was spectacular. I wish I could do a somersault like that but, in my condition, I'm not allowed! He's a lovely lad and couldn't be kinder.'

Her husband Bill, 74, jetted to Portugal to watch his

grandson become a national hero at Euro 2004. He says, 'I'd die happy after seeing that – it makes me cry when I think about him and I go to bed with tears on my pillow. He's dead quiet and shy but he's got the heart of a lion and we've seen him roar.

'When I saw our Wayne run out, my heart went bump, bump. And when he put the ball in the back of that onion bag, it went bumping even more. I was made up. He's a good lad, he's been well brought up, that's the secret. His dad is a wonderful person and so is his mum, my daughter.'

The star is close to his two brothers Graham and John, and just as protective and supportive of them as his parents were of him. He presented an award to boxing-mad Graham at a posh ceremony in Liverpool's Town Hall after the lad became one of the city's most feared junior fighters.

Graham had been nominated for a medal at the Ninth Annual Sporting Honours Awards evening for competing in the international Hancock Boxing Cup in Germany in October 2003.

Wayne, who had himself won a medal for his footballing prowess after representing England at youth level just two years earlier, handed Graham the award at an invitation-only dinner while his parents roared their approval.

The loyal soccer ace was also spotted cheering his brother on at a recent boxing match in Liverpool – and arguing with the referee when a decision went against Graham, climbing up to the ropes and making his feelings clear!

He's since given both his brothers a nest-egg, and treated them to the best money can buy in everything from sporting equipment to Playstations to CD and DVD players.

He says, 'The nice thing about being famous is that I can treat my family. I've been able to buy my mum and dad a house and give them and my brothers some money. I'm really dead pleased to be able to do that. I'll never forget what my parents did for me, I know they made sacrifices. I want to make them proud.'

The doting son has also treated the couple to luxury holidays, including a £10,000 trip to Mexico's upmarket resort of Cancun and a £20,000 two-week cruise around the Caribbean on the luxury *QM2* liner, a surprise gift to his mum for Mother's Day.

But, as far as his dad is concerned, the best gift so far is the £29,025 executive box his son has paid for at Everton's home ground.

The box boasts central heating, air conditioning and is big enough to seat ten, a welcome luxury for those who would otherwise have to spend up to £33 to freeze in a seat in the Lower Gwladys Street stand.

Wayne still spends a majority of his free time in Croxteth, visiting Coleen's parents for tea twice a week, enjoying Sunday lunch with his mum and dad or popping in on his aunts and uncles. If it had been up to him, it's also where he would have celebrated his eighteenth birthday, at the youth centre where he used to play ping-pong as a lad.

But the venue wasn't big enough to hold the 250 guests on his party list, including high-profile soap and pop stars, so it was moved to an executive box at Aintree race-course. Says Wayne, 'Aintree held happy memories for me from when I was a kid. Dad used to take us to watch the horses so it seemed the best place. It was a great day, most of the guests were mine and Coleen's family – there's loads of us, I've got more than 30 cousins living in Croxteth alone – as well as friends from when we were kids.

'It would have been nice to be able to have held the party in Croxteth but the great thing about doing it at Aintree is that I could make it a benefit party for Alder Hey Hospital by inviting loads of celebrities as well.'

The lavish bash, in aid of the Rocking Horse Appeal at Alder Hey, boasted stars from *EastEnders* and *Coronation Street*, Atomic Kitten, as well as team-mates from Everton and England including Francis Jeffers, Alan Stubbs, Michael Owen, Steven Gerrard, Rio Ferdinand and Paul Scholes. David Beckham couldn't make it as he was preparing for a Real Madrid match, but sent a video message.

Ford, who have an advertising deal with the soccer ace, laid on seven Galaxy people carriers, each bearing the legend 'Rooney, Street Striker' and decorated with posters of his face, to ferry guests in and out.

Catering staff had spent two days converting the huge betting hall into a banqueting suite for the mega do, unloading more than 100 bottles of vintage champagne for the thirsty guests.

Wayne's cash-conscious mum had offered to do the grub herself – she knows her son loves her sausage rolls – but the posh nosh at Aintree has won awards and she relented, happy with the menu.

There was still pineapple and cheese on sticks on the buffet table though – Wayne's England mates had joked that they wouldn't turn up unless he asked the catering staff to provide the old-fashioned treat!

The party room was given a New York theme, with a subway train covered in graffiti slogans like 'Roonaldo' and 'Roondog' and 'Wayne 4 Coleen', and an authentic hot dog stand served up the classic American snack.

Above a huge archway were the letters and numbers 'WR 24.10.85', the star's initials and date of birth, and video screens showing childhood pictures of Wayne played throughout the night. Organisers had also erected a 12ft x 12ft TV screen for guests to bet on horse racing around the world at the do.

Wayne and Coleen had shopped in Cheshire's upmarket Wilmslow for their party outfits; he was in a Versace suit from the town's trendy Norton Barrie store and Coleen wore a little black Dolce and Gabbana dress from the Garbo boutique.

The couple arrived at the do each with three generations of their families – cousins, aunts and uncles, grandparents and parents all waving excitedly from the people carriers as they were whisked into the white-tented venue.

They were met by Michelle Ryan and James Alexandrou from *EastEnders*, Atomic Kitten's Liz McLarnon and Busted's James, who had challenged Wayne to a dancing contest later in the evening.

Local bands Rough Hill and Broadway Nites got the party swinging and Wayne's granddad Billy jumped up on stage to sing 'Happy Birthday' to his grandson, joined by the thronging crowd to raise the roof to the star, before Wayne and Coleen presented their mums with flowers.

The star went on to make an emotional speech, thanking his family for their support over the years and officially announcing his engagement to Coleen, making her blush as he wore his heart on his sleeve and paid tribute to his love for her.

Ecstatic Coleen gave her love a diamond and platinum ring and a pair of tickets to see his favourite blue comedian Chubby Brown as gifts – and also a sexy pair of tight-fitting Calvin Klein boxer shorts.

Cheeky Rooney stuck them on straight away and then fell around laughing with his footie pals after realising the boxers were the same type as those donned by Arsenal rival Freddie Ljungberg in a raunchy advert!

Later, as the guests mellowed and the party warmed up, Wayne took to the microphone – the star enjoys singing and insisted that a karaoke machine should be provided at the bash. Says Wayne, 'I sang Oasis' "Supernova", I'm a big fan of theirs, and belted out Robbie Williams's "Let Me Entertain You" as well. I also love dancing – you should see my Michael Jackson robot dance! I did that, too – I cleared the dance floor. James from Busted was dancing with me, we were having a bit of a competition and, of course, I won, there's just no doubt about it, whatever he says! We had everybody round us doing the dance, it was a brilliant laugh.

'Coleen loves dancing, too – she used to go to street jazz dance lessons as a kid – but once I get on the floor she can't keep up, she goes and hides and I always wonder why ...!'

One special guest at the party was 15-year-old Stephen Johnston, a cystic fibrosis sufferer, Everton fan and patient at Alder Hey since his birth. Stephen, who comes from Kirkby, a short hop from Croxteth, met Wayne when the kind-hearted star made several secret visits to the hospital and had promised the excited lad an invite.

The evening went off without a hitch but, best of all, it raised more than £100,000 for the Rocking Horse Appeal at the hospital, a cheque Wayne gladly handed over in a presentation ceremony a few weeks later.

He says, 'The party was great but handing over the cheque was the best bit – it was a brilliant way to celebrate my eighteenth, I was really made up. To be able to do something like that is a privilege and I don't forget that.'

Just five months later, Wayne helped organise Coleen's own eighteenth but, this time, the cocktail of a £10,000 free bar and more than 300 guests proved a tactical error.

Coleen wanted her party kept simple and her mum Colette and dad Tony, who still live on the Croxteth estate, insisted on paying for the bash themselves, as any proud parents would.

The couple hired the £400-a-night Botanic function room at the Devonshire House, a sedate three-star hotel on the edge of the Merseyside estate and conveniently close for most of their relatives.

The evening began well as the guests arrived in high

spirits, a large majority of them members of the Rooney and McCloughlin clans, sprinkled with Wayne's pals from Everton and the couple's childhood friends.

The room had been decorated with pictures of Coleen, showing her growing from childhood through schoolgirl to the cute beauty she has become today, and swathed in the Everton colours of royal blue and white.

It looked stunning, a thoughtful, fitting tribute to Coleen and the man she had chosen to be her future husband – both her parents adore Wayne and he has already become like a son-in-law in their affections, spending much of his youth at their home watching telly with Coleen and her brothers on their sofa.

They are a warm, generous-hearted couple. Colette, a care-worker, and Tony, a former labourer who was forced to abandon his job after a back injury, have often fostered disadvantaged kids despite having three children of their own.

They are both devoted helpers at Claire House in the Wirral, a hospice where their six-year-old daughter Rosie, who suffers from the disabling degenerative condition Rett syndrome, sometimes goes for respite care, and have often accompanied poorly children on trips to the healing waters of Lourdes in France.

The couple have known Wayne's mum and dad for many years – Tony, once a keen amateur boxer, had helped run the gym where Wayne's dad had also boxed and where his children would follow in his footsteps, and both sets of parents had grown up on the Croxteth estate.

The bash was a gathering of the clans, a celebration of

Coleen's birthday but also the fact that the families were now united by the love of Wayne and the girl he had chosen as his future wife.

It was an evening at which emotions ran high, where two sets of proud parents recognised their children achieving adulthood and where wistful reminiscences caused the occasional sentimental tear.

Almost inevitably, as at almost any family do where people are flung together in close proximity with a hefty dose of booze thrown in, the night would end with a drunken scrap. But not before delighted Coleen cut the enormous birthday cake her parents had made, complete with a marzipan figure of herself on top, and a local DJ whipped up the tempo, inviting the happy party-goers to take their turn on the karaoke machine.

One of the first up was Wayne, singing a version of Travis' 'Why Does It Always Rain On Me?' before launching into a romantic Westlife number, his arm round Coleen as he looked into her eyes, making her giggle, before he gave her a beautifully wrapped gift – a £4,000 diamond bracelet.

The couple handed out gifts to their families and Coleen made a speech, thanking her relatives for coming, before the guests took to the dance floor again, Wayne grabbing his fiancée for a smooch as the lights dimmed.

The star had put £10,000 behind the bar, determined Coleen's party should be remembered as every bit as fabulous an occasion as his own had been at Aintree.

As the night wore on, the men took to the karaoke, belting out Everton songs from the terraces, swaying in merry unison and trying, but failing, to get embarrassed Wayne to join in – he might be a star player but the night was Coleen's and he wanted it to stay that way.

By 2.00am, seven hours after the party had started, the booze had run out and the guests were supposed to leave. But, as often happens, some didn't want the fantastic evening to end and the good cheer evaporated when Wayne's tired and emotional uncle, Eugene, jumped on a table, demanding bar staff provide more booze. Chaos ensued, leading to a rumpus as relatives waded in valiantly, trying but failing to cool the soaring, alcohol-fuelled temperature.

Horrified Wayne and Coleen left in tears, the fuming soccer ace distraught that his fiancée's bash had been ruined by the spat and even punching a wall in frustration. Says Wayne, 'I was gutted that Coleen's party was ruined by a few people who couldn't behave. It was just a family party and sometimes things do get heated when people have had too much too drink, but I was still furious.

'There were over 300 guests, friends and family at the party and only a dozen of them could not behave.

'Coleen was heartbroken and I don't mind admitting that I cried, too. I wanted the evening to be special for Coleen – we did have a good time but I was angry that it was spoiled at the end. It's fair to say a few cross words were exchanged later on, everyone was hurt and emotional.'

News of the spat led to claims of a rift between Wayne and his mum and dad and between the two sets of parents – Wayne's dad was even said to have challenged

Coleen's dad to a 'straightener', a boxing match to settle differences.

But says Wayne, 'That's all rubbish. It was just one of this situations you wish had never happened, nothing more. There is no rift or anything like that, it blew over almost as soon as it began. My mum and dad are the people who help me keep my feet on the ground. If I started giving it big time, my dad would just give me a slap!

'He certainly would let me know about it. Even now, if I walk into the house with a new watch, new clothes or whatever, my dad just looks at me and shakes his head. He's just not into clothes and all that stuff. The people closest to me are the ones whose opinions I really take in. They are telling me if I had a bad game. My dad, the manager or my agent will say, "You weren't at your best," or that I could have done better or whatever, so I take all that in.

'I still ask my dad what he thinks because I know he will be straight with me and tell me if I played well or crap. To be honest, I more or less know myself whether I have played well or badly, but I still like to hear their opinion.

'It's important to me and Coleen to be close to our families. What's happened to me, all the fame and that, makes no difference. It is up to me to keep my feet on the ground; if I don't help myself then nobody else can, but it's important to have the support of your family.'

That's one thing Wayne can count on.

His uncle Mark Morrey, 36, also from Croxteth, says, 'One good thing about Wayne is that he is a sensible lad who won't get too big for his boots despite all the madness.

'His mum and dad will keep him firmly on the ground. He knows we're all proud of him but nothing has changed, we're all still the same people he knew as a kid and we all treat him that way.'

Now the family are hoping for another sensational coup. Wayne's cousin James, who teaches singing and dancing at the Gems Youth Centre in Croxteth, says, 'Wayne's brother John is a great footballer, too. I'd say Wayne and John are both better than the Neville brothers already. We are a close family and always in and out of each other's houses, but I'd never play against Wayne and John – they're just too good!

'We won the World Cup in 1966 with two Charlton brothers playing, so there's no telling what the Rooney brothers can do in the future.'

WE We went for a walk ...
we knew we were going to snog.
I took her to the back of the church.
It was the first kiss that ever
mattered to me, she was special.
I knew then that we were made
for each **OTHER**...

4

LOVE MATCH

THE PASSION WHICH burned in Rooney's soul and inspired him to footballing genius had already made him a playground hero, idolised by classmates who would line up to take turns in the break-time kickabouts organised by their star player.

Football was his obsession and occupied his every waking moment but, like many lads embarking on their teenage years, he had another burgeoning interest – girls.

Already standing head and shoulders above his classmates, well-built and with a reputation as a *Boy's Own* hero, Wayne cut an impressive figure on the tough Croxteth council estate he called home.

But he was a bashful lad, quiet and shy. The company of men was his comfort zone, either in the rough and tumble of his uncle's boxing gym, amongst the light-hearted banter of the football changing room or on the testosterone-charged terraces at Everton.

The acne-plagued awkwardness of youth, with limbs and hair sprouting, hormones running wild and emotions sky high, hadn't passed him by.

Wayne couldn't afford to be distracted and, anyway, the cocky charm of the skirt-chaser wasn't in his nature. He was already too streetwise, too thoughtful, too self-aware for that, and counselled by parents who were only too familiar with the pitfalls of estate living. Single motherhood was a fact of life on many of the estate's streets and within in his own family; his dad's favourite pub, The Dog and Gun, on the corner of the road where they lived, had closed down after a police investigation into drug-dealing, and petty vandalism was rife.

The potential for brief but catastrophic youthful fumblings to shatter dreams had also been carefully explained to Wayne at the Everton Academy, where a glittering future now lay within his grasp. Avoiding temptation, confining conquest to the pitch, wised-up Wayne understood the value of cautious discipline.

Still, girls were everywhere, and were moving inexorably closer to his sphere of reference – those he knew as friends, the sisters of his pals, his cousins, his classmates and the beginnings of his adoring fan base. But one girl in particular had captivated the wary lad, his affected boyish indifference slowly evaporating as he came to recognise the unsettling feelings she evoked. Although he didn't know it yet, Wayne was falling in love. And Coleen McLoughlin, the 18-year-old beauty he now plans to wed, was the girl who had captured his heart.

Coleen, a pony-tailed, dark-blonde girl with clear, cat-green eyes, was just 12 years old when she first met Rooney. She was a pupil at the strict, all-girls St John Bosco Roman Catholic School where Wayne's mum Jeanette worked as a part-time cleaner, and was a friend of Claire, the sister of one of the soccer star's favourite cousins Thomas.

It was Thomas's dad Richie who owned the boxing gym where Wayne and his younger brothers Graham and John would often sit and watch football matches on the widescreen telly with their mates, including Coleen's brothers Anthony, now 14, and Joe, now 16.

Eight families from the close-knit Rooney clan were neighbours on the Croxteth estate and the tentacles of their friendships often crossed. Says Coleen, 'I can remember Wayne playing football in the street with my brothers. We were only 12 when we first met and we were all just mates at first.'

Coleen's parents lived a few minutes' walk around the corner from Wayne's family and, like Wayne Sr, her dad had been a keen amateur boxer.

He helped Wayne's uncle Richie to run the boxing gym and had coached young Rooney there as a boy. The families shared in common an earnest Roman Catholic faith and a fierce desire to see their children succeed.

Wayne was comfortable around Coleen. She was a no-nonsense girl who, like him, harboured a driving ambition. Since the age of six, she had wanted to be an actress and, like him, was hard-working and wholly dedicated to her goal.

Says Wayne, 'I had to walk past Coleen's house every day to get to school. Our families knew each other because Coleen's dad helped run the gym where my dad boxed. At that stage, I didn't really know Coleen and I just used to hang around with other lads up the road. Still, by the time I was 14, I knew I fancied her. But Coleen wasn't really interested in boys. She was a goody who did her homework. All I was interested in was football.'

With a maturity beyond their years, both recognised their ambitions would necessitate sacrifice, a fact which became glaringly obvious when Wayne's starburst talent catapulted him into the spotlight on the world stage.

While he dazzled on the pitch in England's 2–0 win over Turkey in England's Euro 2004 qualifier, Coleen remained at home to star as Fat Sam in her school's production of *Bugsy Malone* and, earlier, had stayed behind to sit an English exam while he flew out to join the squad at Spain's La Manga camp for pre-season training.

Even today, as the future wife of England's brightest star, her ambition remains. The lass recently auditioned for a role in *Goal!*, prophetically enough, about a working-class lad who becomes a world-class footballer, and says, 'I've always known I wanted to act and I want to be recognised for what I achieve, not only for being with Wayne.'

The green-shoots of the couple's romance grew from a

steady, innocent friendship, flourishing on the street corners of Croxteth before love begun to bud.

As the afternoon light began to fade, Wayne would often ride out on his mountain bike to fetch paper-wrapped fries from his local chippie, returning to find Coleen sitting on a wall, watching as her brothers and their mates played footie.

He'd plonk himself down beside her, offering her chips with a nonchalance that belied his beating heart. Says Coleen, 'We used to spend hours hanging around on the street corner, just talking to each other. At first, we were just mates but then we began to spend more time together and we became best friends – Wayne knows me better than anyone else.'

But Wayne was too shy to ask Coleen for a formal date. She was the girl-next-door he'd known since childhood, an ambitious, bright girl he counted as a trusted friend. He was uncertain whether the tender affection he felt towards her would be returned and, in a quandary, played the joker to try and gauge her feelings. The star admits, 'I used to pull little stunts to try and get close to her because, until I know people, I can be quite shy. I desperately wanted to kiss her but I didn't know how. I remember once I pretended to have contact lenses that I couldn't get in my eyes and asked her to have a look and see if my eyes were OK.

'I could never get the courage to ask her out properly or kiss her. I used to try and ask but she wouldn't take it seriously. I invited her out on loads of dates – to the chippie, the pictures, I even promised to take her to Paris for Valentine's Day if she'd come on a date.

'She was gorgeous-looking, had a great personality, but she always thought I was skitting her.'

It wasn't until Wayne turned knight in shining armour, riding to the rescue after spotting his princess in trouble, that he managed to win his date – and, then, only after enlisting the help of Claire, his cousin and Coleen's friend.

He said, 'My day came when the chain came off Coleen's bike. She was with my cousin Claire and I saw them trying to fix it. I was on my way home and stopped to help. I used it as an excuse to chat to Coleen, asking if I could borrow her video of *Grease* – I've always been a fan. I loved that movie and knew she did, too.

'When Coleen went inside to get the video, I grabbed Claire and asked her to get Coleen to come on a date with me. By then, I was fed up of asking. But this time, Coleen said yes!'

The couple shyly walked across the street, Wayne's heart thudding as he knew his moment had come – he was going to steal a kiss off the girl he adored. Carefully, he steered her towards the church, a place well known as a local lovers' lane where young sweethearts met for secret snogs. Said Wayne, 'We went for a walk … we knew we were going to snog. I took her to the back of the church. It was the first kiss that ever mattered to me, she was special. I knew then that we were made for each other but I was lost for words. Coleen did most of the talking – I think she was shocked at what a fantastic kisser I was!

'I walked her home and I phoned her as soon as I got in and asked her for a proper date. The next day, we planned to go out. I'd arranged to meet my friends in

town and I was so excited I bought a whole new outfit —
a green jumper, jeans and brown shoes.'

The couple went to the Showcase Cinema, a frayed,
old-fashioned picture house just a short stroll from their
homes, to see *Austin Powers: International Man of
Mystery*, followed by cheeseburger and chips at a fast-
food restaurant close by.

It was their first proper, unchaperoned date and
Wayne walked her home, a shy acknowledgement
between them that, now, they were officially an item.
'We realised we liked each other more than just mates,'
is how Coleen puts it. 'When I first started seeing him, I
was a bit nervous and we kept it secret. I never told my
dad if I kissed a lad, he is quite protective.'

Wayne was formally introduced to Coleen's family at
a christening gathering for her cousin's baby. Coleen
said, 'Wayne wore jeans and a shirt — everybody loved
him. I expected my dad to be more protective but he
was quite relaxed because Wayne had been coming
round so much and he knew his dad from boxing.'

The coals of the sweethearts' passion were ignited,
but their romance was forced to burn slowly as Wayne's
meteoric rise to stardom took off.

He was just 16, earning £90 a week at Everton, when
he hung up his De La Salle school uniform for the last
time at Easter.

Just seven months later, on his seventeenth birthday,
he became a fully fledged member of the Everton élite,
signing his first professional contract and becoming one
of the richest youngsters in world football, earning up to
£18,000 a week, including bonuses.

The three-year deal – the maximum length of time for a 17-year-old – made him the highest-paid teenager in Everton's history, earning the kind of mind-boggling money each week that those from his home turf in Croxteth rarely saw in a year.

The fuse of superstardom had been lit, the football world fizzing with excitement as Rooney scored goal after sensational goal for the club's youth team. A £2 million endorsement deal with Nike plopped through the letterbox just weeks later, signed with a trembling flourish by the disbelieving lad.

Coleen had celebrated her sixteenth birthday on 3 April 2002, just a few weeks before Wayne had left De La Salle School. So certain was he that she'd remain a permanent fixture in his life, he'd even had her name tattooed on his right arm.

Again, he'd taken her to the cinema before they enjoyed her birthday outing to Liverpool's trendy 051 club, Wayne sipping a shandy while she stuck to Coke, before taking a taxi back and lingering by the wall near her home, chatting amiably and excitedly about Wayne's prospects, until the front door opened and her mum called her in.

Her parents were strict about time-keeping, anxious that she should prepare for the exacting A-levels she was due to begin at St John Bosco sixth-form in September, and determined that what might be no more than a fleeting teenage infatuation should not distract their clever daughter from her studies.

But Wayne already knew Coleen was the girl for him. He says, 'I'd stopped going out with my mates as much, although I still played football before I saw her every night! I just wanted to be with her.'

As Wayne wandered slowly home, his mind quietly ticking over, he felt a bubble of happiness well inside and smiled – he knew Coleen was the girl he wanted to marry. It was just a matter of time before he'd let her know. It never once occurred to him that the whole world would want to know, too.

But that moment, the moment when Wayne would shake the football world to its foundations and become a global superstar, was just around the corner.

Destiny would come knocking, first in the momentous signing for his beloved Everton and then, with fairytale unreality, in the form of England manager Sven-Göran Eriksson.

Rooney, instantly promoted to the Toffees' first-team squad and handed the number 18 shirt previously sported by Paul Gascoigne, took just weeks to smash his way into Everton's record books.

On 24 September, in a bitterly contested match against Wrexham, the teenage powerhouse became Everton's youngest ever scorer, sent on as a sub to belt home two astonishing goals in the Worthington Cup win.

But it was his spectacular last-minute goal against Arsenal a month later which left the football world open-mouthed, drooling at the sheer, audacious brilliance of the boy, a boy still five days short of his seventeenth birthday.

It was a goal which saw world-class 'keeper David Seaman, the England squad's safe pair of hands, left sitting helplessly on his backside – and saw Rooney become the Premiership's youngest ever scorer.

An awe-inspiring legend was being carved on the hallowed pitches of England's Premiership clubs – and, just a few months later, the whole world would hear the story.

Knock, knock ...

Who's there?

Sven ...

His début match against Australia at Upton Park in February 2003 was a humiliating defeat for England, a 3–1 scoreline to the Socceroos sending hearts plummeting, especially since the Three Lions had been odds-on favourites to win.

But a hero emerged from the depressing ashes of defeat – Rooney, England's youngest ever player at the age of 17 years and 111 days, had outperformed some of the nation's biggest football names, his place in the galaxy of soccer's greats already assured.

He'd played alongside his heroes, men he'd cheered wildly as a schoolboy, sitting in the front room of his gran's council house, willing England to victory.

His name was on everyone's lips. Suddenly, the world was his oyster, people clamouring to congratulate and celebrate with the new-born star. But there was just one place he wanted to be – back at home, on the proud-as-punch streets of Croxteth, with the girl he loved.

The thrill of his record-breaking game still coursing through his veins, Wayne dashed back to share his first moments of glory with Coleen and was dropped off at her parents' home by a friend – an England star he may have been, but he still hadn't passed his driving test.

Later, as twilight blanketed the ragged Croxteth skyline, he shared a bag of chips, a bottle of Coke and a kickabout in the street with his mates, just an ordinary evening for the extraordinary boy who had the world at his feet.

It would be the last time he'd need to buy his own Coke – within weeks, Rooney had signed up with Coleen to front a £500,000 advertising campaign with the fizzy drinks giant, a team effort like Posh and Becks before them.

And, just a month later, the lad who had worn hand-me-down trainers was revelling in the luxurious surrounds of the England training camp at La Manga, a million miles from the caravan in a Welsh holiday park near Rhyl where he'd spent childhood holidays with his cousins, the boys booting their way to glory on a tufted square of sun-baked grass which served as their stadium.

La Manga was a name he knew, famous as the base for England's pre-season training and frequently linked in newspaper headlines with tales of drunken antics and high jinks among the pampered players.

And here he was, about to join the serried ranks of England shirts at La Manga, his dream of playing in the Euro 2004 qualifiers just a few weeks from becoming reality.

La Manga, a five-star resort where the scent of money wafted lazily across the manicured lawns, spoke of exotic luxuries Wayne had only ever brushed up against in the pages of glossy magazines, left carelessly discarded in the players' lounge at Everton for others to flick through aimlessly.

It held few mysteries, though. He'd been carefully coached from an early age by the team at Everton's Academy and taken under the wing of Alan Stubbs, now 32, a senior club player, who'd ensured the boy from the backstreets was well steeped in the polish which would help him blend in.

But for Coleen, still every inch a schoolgirl, the very thought of setting foot in the place was enough to stir the kind of frantic anxiety any woman feels on her first foray into unknown sophistication, never mind a sixth-form student from the tough streets of Crocky. 'I didn't know what to expect. I was dead scared,' she says.

The couple's relationship was now a firm fixture. Wayne had been welcomed into Coleen's family, staying at their home overnight to share tender moments with his girl. He says, 'Coleen had a TV and video in her bedroom and we'd go upstairs together to watch things like *Grease* or *Armageddon*. I remember I told Coleen I loved her first. We were watching *Pearl Harbour*, sitting on the sofa at her house. I just told her I loved her. I think the film was a bit of an emotional one and it just came over me!

'Even when I used to go home, which was just down the road, I'd phone her as soon as I got in the door to tell her I was back. Then I'd text her to tell her I loved her, and I'd often pick her up from school.'

The rock-solid relationship met with the approval of Coleen's mum and dad. They recognised Wayne's serious intent – and their daughter's love for him – and agreed to allow Coleen to make her first trip alone with Wayne to La Manga.

It would be the first time she'd flown alone – Coleen had to sit an English exam on the day the squad flew out, joining her hero a day later. And she was petrified! She remembers, 'I rang Wayne and asked him to find out what kind of clothes the women were wearing. I told him to look when they came down for breakfast, but he told me everyone had eaten in their rooms. I was really worried I would take the wrong clothes or not know what to do.'

Just a few months earlier, she'd decked herself out in a simple powder-blue top and white jeans to celebrate her seventeenth birthday with Wayne at the Kung Fu Chinese restaurant in St Helens, five miles away from the house she still shared with her parents. The couple had feasted on vegetable spring rolls, mixed vegetable chow mein and sweet and sour chicken with fried rice, washed down with Coke, before Wayne paid the £40 bill.

Later, delighted Coleen unwrapped her sweetheart's gift, a £6,000 Marc Jacobs watch, soon to be replaced that Christmas with an £18,000 diamond-encrusted, platinum Rolex, de rigueur amongst the glitterati at La Manga.

But now, with her flat, black shoes, short socks, lumpy padded anorak and skin devoid of make-up, Coleen, a rucksack slung across her shoulders, was still the kind of everyday girl who could be spotted at school bus-stops across the nation.

She was relying on her man to come up with the vital information on the wardrobe requirements. But, like a typical bloke, Wayne couldn't understand what all the fuss was about. Clad casually in T-shirt and shorts as he roamed the upmarket resort, he still hadn't completed his spy mission by the time nerve-wracked Coleen was boarding her plane from Britain.

'When I got to the airport, I rang him again to find out and he still didn't know,' she says. 'Luckily, when I arrived, I had brought the right clothes!'

A resourceful girl, Coleen, like her friends, had spent many hours on dreary, rainy days poring over pictures of the high-maintenance women often found draped on the arms of footballers and pop stars.

An express shopping trip with her mum around the designer stores of Manchester, a short hop from Liverpool and boasting a posh Harvey Nichol's, secured the glitzy dresses, sunglasses and trendy red Burberry bikini which would see her elevated to cover-girl status from the minute she touched down on her sun lounger.

She says, 'My mum rang me to tell me there were pictures of me all over the newspapers. I couldn't believe it – I was dead worried what I looked like in my bikini!'

She needn't have worried. The girl Wayne affectionately called 'Babe' looked gorgeous, a refreshing change from the sleekly expensive artifice surrounding her, and was soon the tabloid's darling, her natural curves, dewy young skin and innocent charm elbowing Victoria Beckham off the front pages.

At first, naturally, Coleen was overawed by the world-famous celebrities around her. Surreally, people she'd only ever seen in pictures sat beside her at breakfast, chattering with their families about plans for the day over freshly baked croissants, at ease and at home in the plush surroundings.

Liverpool's striker Michael Owen, his baby daughter Gemma nestled in his arms, lounged in the sun with his partner Louise Bonsall, sharing a joke with Wayne.

Steven Gerrard, also a hero-worshipped Red, and his stunning girlfriend Alex, soaked up the 80°F heat nearby, teasing the couple with Scouse humour and beginning a bond which would later see him become a pal to Rooney as the lad sweltered under the unwavering glare of the spotlight.

Queen bee Victoria Beckham offered the hand of friendship, inviting Coleen to spend the day with the girls while the boys sloped off for a game of golf, a first for Wayne but, inevitably, not a last, or to challenge each other at go-karting.

Soon, Coleen was gossiping away with the rest of them, relaxed in sleeveless T-shirt — the royal blue of Everton, of course — and grey camouflage shorts as she absorbed the buzz of conversation around her.

'Victoria was chatting away, she was lovely,' says Coleen, 'but I mostly hung out with Steven Gerrard, Jamie Carragher and Michael Owen and their girlfriends because we're all from Liverpool. I would like a little of what Victoria has, her clothes and look,' adds Collen, 'but I don't see her as someone to look up to because I think everyone should be their own person.'

Alone, at night, she snuggled up with Wayne to

watch *Only Fools and Horses* on a DVD player, dissecting the day before joining their new-found celebrity friends at dinner.

It was the stuff dreams are made of, the dreams of little boys and girls who weave feverish fantasies as they fall into slumber, knowing they'll never likely come true. But, for the very lucky, talented and select few, those dreams do come true.

'I have to pinch myself to believe what's happened to Wayne,' said Coleen, 'but nobody deserves it more.'

The couple's love affair found breathing space on their first holiday alone, an eye-opening adventure in America's Miami, lazing on the beach and soaking up the atmosphere in one of the USA's most celebrated playgrounds.

It was there, during blissful sun-soaked days, that love blossomed from courtship to commitment. The rosy hue of a future marriage hung in the air and, just a week later, the couple joined both their families in the smart Mexican resort of Cancun.

Says Wayne, 'It was a dream holiday compared to those when I was little, but we were young and thought we might be bored on our own, so we invited our parents to join us in Mexico. We had a villa and we asked Coleen's dad if we could share a room. Coleen was nervous asking her dad, but it was all right.

'I was a bit awkward at first, too. I didn't know what her dad was going to come out with, because he has a dry sense of humour. My parents came as well and they didn't mind at all. They didn't give us the speech about safe sex, we were old enough to know about that.

'Coleen's mum had chatted to her about it, but not in

a big lecture kind of way. We knew we wanted to be together and stay together.'

But, while affairs of the heart were rapidly fermenting, the siren song of Rooney's first love was calling and, on 6 September 2003, he answered with a passion which took the nation's breath away.

Another record toppled as Wayne became the youngest England player ever to score in a full international, netting the first goal in a 2–1 Euro 2004 qualifier against Macedonia. Coleen, who had just returned to school to start her A-levels, had to be content with watching her lover shoot his way to victory on the TV at home.

'My whole family were at our house to watch the game,' she says. 'I rang Wayne the day before and said to him, "Are you going to score for me today?" and he said, "Yes!" When the goal went in, I couldn't believe it. I was rooted to the spot for a moment, I didn't think or do anything. Then, when it sank in, I jumped out of my chair and started screaming and cheering.

'My dad's a Liverpool supporter but the whole family were leaping around and hugging each other. I was so proud of him.'

Wayne later admitted he was just as gobsmacked, so blinded by euphoria he didn't know what to do or where to run after he'd scored.

Rooney may have been just 17 years old but, with the same certainty that had directed his boots, he knew where his romantic heart lay and, just a month later, the soccer star formally proposed to his sweetheart – on the forecourt of a BP garage!

Says Wayne, 'I had the ring made to my design. It's

platinum and diamond, I know what she likes. Coleen had tried to interfere but she made it to complicated!

'I'd picked it up from the jeweller and told her we were going out for a Chinese meal, but we stopped at a BP petrol garage to get money from the cashpoint.

'When she was getting the cash, I got the box out of my pocket and had it open. She got back into the car and I asked, "Will you marry me?"

'She was a bit emotional, she said "Yes" and we had a bit of a hug. Asking Coleen to marry me was worse than walking out for England.

'We didn't bother going for that meal. We rang Coleen's mum and told her to get the dinner on and went back to watch *EastEnders*. Coleen couldn't wait to get back and show everybody her ring. She loves it. When we got there, her mum had put candles on the table. It was really special.

'We'd already discussed getting married a few months earlier. We knew we were only young but Coleen talked to her mum and she was happy for us. So were my parents when we spoke to them, too. But I was determined to ask her dad properly.

'I'll never forget the night. We were all sat in the living room watching TV and her dad already knew what was on my mind because her mum had told him.

'Eventually, after four hours of awkward silence, he finally said, "Haven't you got something to say to me, Wayne?"

'I said, "Can I marry your daughter, please?" Then he gave me a big lecture and said, "If you love each other, I give my blessing."

'Then he told me to look after her but said it was two people from the same area who loved each other and he knew it was right. Finally, he shook my hand and her mum started crying.'

Even better, just a few weeks earlier, Wayne had passed his driving test – on his third attempt – and the couple could seek the privacy they craved away from the bright lights of Liverpool. Says Coleen, 'If we go out for dinner or out shopping, we get a lot of people coming up to us. So we mostly went to the cinema because it was dark and no one could see who Wayne was. Even now, we do our shopping at Tesco at 10.00pm, because we're less likely to see many people. When Wayne passed his driving test, it made things a lot easier.

'He was very nervous when he proposed. People think we are too young but I don't think we are. It is up to the individual … I know the time is right. He is the person I love and want to stay with for the rest of my life. It's not up to anyone else.

'We haven't set a date yet. I actually feel too young to do that. I want it to be beautiful and really well planned. A wedding only comes once, so I want it to be dead special. We can be engaged for years so there's plenty of time to make wedding plans.'

Wayne, unafraid to wear his heart on his sleeve, says simply, 'She's a nice girl to be around and I wanted to make sure I keep her around.'

Just a few weeks later, Wayne moved in with Coleen's parents after buying his own mum and dad a £470,000 home in Liverpool's upmarket West Derby. He says,

'Mum and Dad were moving and getting their house sorted so I moved in with Coleen's parents. I was virtually living there anyway – I spent most evenings at her house!'

By November, the couple were enjoying the kind of high-profile celebrity lifestyle common amongst the footballing élite, canoodling in a VIP area at a Beyoncé Knowles concert and, later, Coleen waltzing down the catwalk in a red mini-dress, raising cash at a charity fashion show.

Within a few weeks, she'd signed up with Wayne's influential agent Paul Stretford, landed a small part in Merseyside soap *Hollyoaks* and quit her A-level studies. Says Coleen, 'I just felt doing A-levels then wasn't right for me. I was getting offered acting parts but I couldn't take them because of my school work. I'd like to go to drama school, maybe to university, but there's plenty of time to do that. At the moment, I'm just looking after our new home.'

The lovebirds finally enjoyed their first night alone on Valentine's Day 2004, enjoying chocolates and champagne at Liverpool's Marriott Hotel, a lavishly restored art-deco building which was formerly an old-fashioned airport terminal. Says Wayne, 'We were going to a party and, halfway through the night, I asked Coleen, "Should I phone your dad and ask if we can stay out?"

'He said "Yes", so I booked a room at the Marriott Hotel in Liverpool. We arrived at about 1.00am and there was champagne and chocolates already there. It was a fantastic night, our first full night completely alone together.'

Just a month later, the couple would leave behind the streets of Croxteth to move into their new £1.3 million mansion in Formby, a 20-minute drive from the council estate which had spawned their love – and which will always be home in their hearts.

I had to go training five nights
a week ... During the week, I
wouldn't get home until 9.30pm,
too late to play with my friends.
They would be going to the cinema
or hanging out in the street together,
and I'd be putting on my kit to train.
There were times I didn't want to
go, I just wanted to give it all UP.

5

FOOTBALLER'S COMING HOME

THE ROON OF *the Rovers* story has only just begun but, already, the magic in the boy's boots has transformed his life for ever.

The star, still just 18 years old but earning more than £1 million a year, now lives in a five-bedroom mansion in Liverpool's upmarket Formby, nestling in leafy grounds on the local millionaire's row. It's a short walk from the seaside, and boasts a mini-cinema, swimming pool and games room where Wayne and his fiancée Coleen often challenge their brothers to snooker matches.

Decorated in neutral creams and beiges, the Italian furniture is plush and the best money can buy – the couple spent £50,000 in one shopping trip at swanky Manchester store Stockton's, where a single sofa can set you back £25,000.

Neighbours include Everton team-mates Duncan

Ferguson and Alan Stubbs, who helped the couple choose their new home – bought for £900,000 as an investment and paid for in cash in February 2004; it's already worth £1.3 million.

At present, Wayne drives a sporty version of the £10,000 Ford Ka, part of a sponsorship deal with the car giant but, recently, he sat his advanced driving test, learning to handle luxury fast cars. The SportKa is hardly in keeping with his glamorous lifestyle – most high-profile footballers have at least a Ferrari, Aston Martin or Porsche sitting on the driveway. But Wayne wants to be sensible. He says, 'I'm only 18, haven't been driving very long and I don't think I'm ready for a very fast car. The main thing is, I don't want to damage my car or put myself in danger, so why risk it just to drive fast?

'I always stick to the speed limit – my mates do try to get the car off me and show what it can really do, they're a bit wilder than me! The car is nippy, it's great for getting round the streets in Liverpool – and you do still get the looks. I know what it's like to be a woman now, pretending you haven't seen lads checking you out!

'I haven't had a crash yet, touch wood, but there was a time I was going training at Bellefield and there were loads of fans at the gate. So I had to go wide to get around them and ended up missing the turn – I couldn't turn sharp enough to go through the gate.

'I had to reverse to get in, it was really embarrassing! If I was going to get a fast car it would probably be a Jag or a Ferrari, but I'm happy with my nippy little number for the moment.

'On my CD player in the car I have the Stereophonics, Travis and Tupac Shakur, especially the track "Hit 'Em Up", played loud. I've got S Club Juniors in my glovebox, but it's my girlfriend's ... honest! On the way to Goodison I listen to Radio City, a local Liverpool station, and, after a match, I try to catch the football phone-in.'

Ford are also responsible for Jaguar, which means a 146mph X-type saloon, which will burn a £26,000 hole in your pocket, could soon be taking pride of place on Wayne's driveway.

The couple's childhood holidays to Spanish apartments on the Costa del Sol in Spain or to a caravan park in Wales are no more than fond memories now, replaced by frolicking on white-sand beaches during lavish holidays to luxury resorts like Mexico's Cancun or Florida's Miami coastline. It's the stuff long-cherished dreams are made of, the kind of lottery-winner lifestyle which prompts millions to buy a £1 ticket each week in the hope that they might live it.

Yet Wayne and Coleen are still teenagers, thrust suddenly into the glare of the spotlight, plucked from the familiar, pock-marked streets of a council estate and plonked in the middle of a pristine fairytale smattered with gold.

Adapting to the radical change in their lifestyle hasn't been easy. Coleen, still just 18, had never before been away from her family home for more than a few days. She's a shy, endearingly easy-going girl, bashful but strong-minded and still wavering on the cusp between child and woman. Her lifelong dream of becoming an actress has been put on the back burner after she quit her A-levels to remain at Wayne's side, the pressure of his stardom already weighing heavily on her.

Jealous girls at her school had started bitching and, on top of the intense scrutiny of her every move, Coleen decided her safest place was with the man she loves and the couple moved into their new home just a few months after she ditched her studies at St John Bosco School.

But adjusting to the unfamiliar surroundings of the posh neighbourhood and the wrench away from the safe haven of her childhood home has naturally been unsettling. Says Wayne, 'Coleen went to see the house first and she loved it, so then we went together and, when I saw it, I knew it was the place for us. But, when we first moved in, it was weird, so big and empty. I remember Coleen's mum crying because she was going to miss her so much but I had always wanted a house of my own and I wanted Coleen to live with me.

'It's not been so difficult for me, because I've been used to going away from my family for training and to play in competitions and staying in hotels. But it's a lot for Coleen, she's just 18, and to have a house like ours of her own is a lot on her shoulders.

'Coleen still can't sleep on her own. Where we lived before, her house was on a main road and there was always the noise of traffic, but where we are now is very quiet, you could hear a pin drop.

'She gets scared, so we've got a dog, a chow called Fizz. I take Coleen up to bed, and I watch a DVD while she falls asleep.'

Wayne scores for England in the 2–0 game against Liechtenstein on 10 September 2003.

Wayne displays the BBC Young Sports Personality of the Year Award in December 2002.

Top: Wayne arrives at Everton's Bellefield training ground in his car on his birthday.

Bottom: England team-mates Michael Owen (middle) and Steven Gerrard (far right) and Wayne take rather less powerful vehicles for a spin on the golf course.

Top Left: Everton play Newcastle United on 6 April 2003. Everton won 2–1, one goal scored by Wayne.

Top Right: The Young Sports Personality of the Year faces Liverpool on 22 December 2002 in what would turn out to be a goal-free draw.

Bottom: David Moyes congratulates Wayne on the victory over Newcastle.

Top left: Delight at scoring against Macedonia. England beat Macedonia 2–1 on 6 September 2003.

Top right: Wayne celebrates scoring England's first goal with team mates.

Bottom left: Hotly pursued by Bolton's Bruno N'Gotty (far right), Wayne boots one over the bar in a November 2003 game. Bolton win 2–0.

Bottom right: In action at what would be a goalless draw against Manchester City in December 2003.

Euro 2004: during the match against Croatia which England went on to win 4–2 on 21 June 2004.

Top: Disaster! Jeanette and Wayne Snr watch in horror as their son is brought down in the dramatic match against Portugal on 24 June 2004.

Bottom left: A sad return for Coleen to Manchester airport the day after Wayne's injury.

Bottom right: Wayne limps back home, arriving at Manchester airport.

Wayne and Coleen board a plane in May 2004.

Wayne is immensely protective of Coleen and clearly hopelessly in love with her. He's careful to drape a reassuring arm around her when they're in company and is unselfconscious about the unabashed affection he feels for her, tenderly stroking her leg or the side of her face without hesitation.

They look to each other constantly for approval, she shyly under her lashes while his knowing blue eyes meet hers with a steady, piercing gaze. It's clear there is a deep bond between them, born of an enduring friendship and the kind of unflinching intimacy which can only grow over time. Wayne is unashamedly besotted and doesn't care who knows it, his gaze only ever momentarily straying from the 5ft 2in girl snuggled by his side.

He worries for her, because he recognises with an acute and unexpected awareness that she is coping with the pressures of fame, because of him and for him. He says, 'I want Coleen to be happy – that makes me happy. It worries me that she might feel lonely at the house when I'm training or whatever, so I'm always encouraging her to go out shopping or to see her mates. I want her to enjoy her life … what I'm doing is for us, not just me. We're a team, that's the way it is, and I want for her to be happy. She's the most special person in my life. Coleen's not just beautiful on the outside, but she's beautiful on the inside as well.

'She's gorgeous-looking but she's also got a great personality, she's a dead special person and I can't think of another person who is a patch on my Coleen. From the moment I first kissed her – I was just 14 – I always knew she was the girl for me and that feeling never changed, it just stayed strong and I enjoy every moment with her.'

Coleen is spending her time turning the mansion into an intimate home, buying furniture and dealing with teams of workmen who are currently building a dressing room for her.

She says, 'That's my priority at the moment. I would like to go back to drama school and act in the future, but Wayne and I haven't had much time to settle into the house, what with training for the Euro 2004 tournament and then going out to the tournament itself. I've had it decorated in creams and beiges, it's quite plain and calm, and now it's just trying to get all the rest of the stuff done.'

In the dining room, a vast picture of Wayne scoring his first goal for England – against Macedonia in September 2003 – takes pride of place across one wall. He says, 'It's my most treasured possession. All the players and staff for England have signed it. Michael wrote, "That's another one of my records you have broken," and Steven Gerrard put, "Well done, ugly arse!"'

Rooney's cousin Thomas remembers only too well the moment Wayne returned to the streets of Croxteth as an international star. He says, 'Wayne hasn't changed at all, he just does normal things. He just rings up and asks us what we are up to and comes round to chat. That's what he did after playing for England against Macedonia. The only difference was, we all wanted to know about the players. We were like, "What's Beckham like?" "What about the others?" Wayne just said, "Yeah, OK." He was too shy to ask for autographs, but he did get us Alan Shearer's.

'It's amazing Wayne meets all these people now when, just a while ago, we all had their posters on our wall. It's mad.'

While the couple grow accustomed to living away from their childhood homes for the first time in their lives, it's their families who are providing an invaluable support network. Says Wayne, 'Neither me nor Coleen are very domesticated. Coleen does the washing and her mum comes round and irons and hoovers. If I leave anything on the floor, Coleen goes mad, but then, when she is going out with the girls, she goes out in one outfit and leaves about 50 on the floor! We do argue about that, just silly things like that.

'We still go to Coleen's mum for dinner a couple of times a week and she does a great spaghetti bolognese or fish because she knows I like it. We visit my mum and dad or my aunts and cousins every week, too, and we always have a family roast back in Croxteth each Sunday.'

The couple are determined to stay close to their roots, anxious that the glitterball of fame shouldn't distract them from what is most important in their lives. They've witnessed how easy it is to become a casualty of fame, the lesson of the brilliant Paul Gascoigne, himself a former Everton player and subsequently an alcoholic, never far from their minds. Says Wayne, 'Sometimes, when I glance back, I think everything has happened so fast. I suppose you could look at Gazza. His footballing career was unbelievable for ten years but he had problems off the pitch. I don't think that will happen to me. I am a normal lad, who likes watching TV and being with his fiancée. We have a glass of wine but we're not into heavy drinking or going out to loads of nightclubs. Our ideal night is at a family party or going for a nice meal. A usual night for us is watching *EastEnders* and *Corrie* and then going to bed, where I'll watch the DVD and Coleen falls asleep.

'She thinks 10.00pm is late, but then she has to get me up for training with a cuppa because I hate getting out of bed, and to walk the dog. We're still in touch with our mates from school. Two of my best mates are Bradley and John who I've known since primary school. They come round to our house a couple of times a week and stay over. We get a DVD, a glass of wine, an Italian takeaway and just sit around and chat.

'It is really funny because Bradley, who is a printer, is an Everton fan and John, who is a builder, is a Liverpool fan.

'They sit and argue about the football teams but I'm not allowed to join in. If I try to say anything, they say, "Shut up, what do you know anyway?"

'We never discuss football, I can't get a word in edgeways. They help keep me grounded … it would be impossible to get big-headed around them.

'Some people did change towards me when I started playing for England, mates who got scared to skit me, as if I had changed. And then there were people I thought were mates who asked me for signed shirts to keep but, when I went round to their houses later, I found they had sold them on the Internet. I was really disappointed by that.

'But not Bradley and John. They treat me the same as they did when we were kids. I know they are secretly impressed, though, because they have both got signed posters of me on their bedroom walls – and shirts, too.

'I also have mates from Everton – Duncan Ferguson, who was always my idol as a kid, and Alan Stubbs. Alan is the player I am probably closest to. He comes round to our house quite often and I'll ring him if something is bothering me. When I was with the Everton youth team, he used to pick me up and drive me home.

'They call me "The Dog" at the club – I've been called that since I was 13. They used to call me Wayne but then it suddenly changed and I still don't know why it's The Dog.

'Alan came round to our house recently and was standing at the bottom of the stairs, shouting, "Dog, dog, are you there, dog?" There were workmen in the house and the door was open so he'd just wandered straight in. Coleen and I were still asleep. It took Alan a bit of an embarrassing while to explain to the workmen that he was looking for me – they thought he had come to walk our dog Fizz. I was killing myself laughing upstairs!'

Wayne has a reputation as a shy boy, a youngster who needs to let his magic boots do the talking and with an aggressive edge born of his upbringing on the back streets.

But it couldn't be further from the truth. Meet him in the flesh, and it's a revelation – warm, funny and extrovert, Wayne could talk the hind leg off a donkey – and does! He enjoys nothing more than sending himself up and is refreshingly honest when it comes to wearing his heart on his sleeve. There's no artifice to Rooney – what you see is what you get. And what you get is a charming, streetwise lad with a sharp wit and shrewd eyes.

He may be a powerhouse on the pitch, a presence so electrifying he seems to fill the TV screen, tackling his foes with the type of bulldozing ruggedness which makes him seem a bulldog. But, surprisingly, he's just 5ft 10in and, despite his broad shoulders, is no man mountain. He's about as threatening as a pussycat – and just as playful, sending himself up mercilessly. He says, 'People think I'm this shy boy, but when you get to know me I can actually be quite loud. I do take a while to come out of my shell, I don't jump in feet first when I meet people, I'm quite cautious.'

But, he says with a grin, he has hidden talents off the pitch – and mocking himself is one of them. He says, 'I'm a lad whose Michael Jackson impression can clear the dance floor – and I can sing like Will Young! I've always loved singing. I'm always saying to Coleen if I hadn't been a footballer I would have got into the last ten of *Pop Idol*.

'Coleen can laugh – and she does. But I know it's only because I am such a fantastic singer. I'll often sing to her in the morning, usually something by Usher ... it's the music I use to psyche myself up before a game. Or I'll belt out a bit of Robbie Williams's "Let Me Entertain You" or something by Will Young.

'When I was a kid, I had a karaoke machine in my bedroom and I'd stand there in front of the mirror, singing a slushy Westlife number or the Stereophonics.

'I also love 50 Cent, Eminem … and Lionel Richie is another favourite. Sometimes, I don't quite get the high pitch but I still like to practise – as a kid, even with a hairbrush when there was no microphone to hand!

'I also enjoy a good dance. In fact, I bought a Michael Jackson DVD so I could practise my moves at home before we went to Euro 2004 – and my moonwalk is as brilliant as ever!'

Rooney, his foot in plaster after he was injured during the Portugal–England clash at Euro 2004, adds with a grin, 'I would show you, Sue, only my foot's hurting …!'

At heart, Rooney is a teenager and, like any teenager, he has the same interests and unease at carrying a heavy weight of expectation.

He's a decent lad, a credit to his Liverpool roots and parents – and, while he may have broad shoulders, the idea that he's a hero sits uncomfortably on them.

He still enjoys a game of ping-pong with his cousins or just larking around with his mates. Until a year ago, he still had Alan Shearer's poster on his bedroom wall, along with that of his Everton hero Duncan Ferguson and pop stars J-Lo and Britney Spears.

The England squad may have become close, 'almost like a family', but it's the fans who are the parents, willing Rooney on to ever-greater success.

And given the enormous pressure, like everybody, he's bound to make mistakes as he grows up. His resilience will be tested to the full in the coming months and years as he comes to terms with the fact that the world will hang on his every word and move – and tackle him if he gets it wrong.

He says, 'Just a year ago, I could still go out in the streets and play footie with my mates, but I can't now, everyone wants to join in. When we go out, I am constantly asked for autographs, which I don't mind, but we also get girls coming up and targeting me because I'm a footballer.

'Coleen doesn't say anything because, if she does, she knows she will look like the bad person in the end. Fame does mean we can't always live a normal life ... We have people sitting outside our house in cars, and I don't like that. Sometimes it gets to me, but neither of us would complain, because that's the price you have to pay, it comes with the job and the nice thing about it is that you can treat your friends and family and you get to see some amazing places.

'The great thing is I can go back to Croxteth and people don't treat me differently there. They just look up and think, Oh, it's our Wayne, and walk on by. Even when I walk past the school or get out of the car at Coleen's parents' house, I don't get bothered. People are just used to me being around.

'The thing is, my circumstances have changed, but I haven't. I am still the same person inside, still enjoy the same things. I am still the boy who kicked a ball around in the street. That's not going to change and nor am I. I am still Wayne Rooney, still have the same feelings and like doing the same things. All that has changed is the amount of attention I get. That's been a bit difficult, coping with people who think I'm not still me, that I've somehow become someone else.'

Much has been said in newspapers, magazines and

TV documentaries about Rooney's new-found wealth and the luxuries it has bought him. But none of it came easy. He says, 'Sometimes, people seem to imagine I have won the lottery or something, as if everything has just happened for me overnight and that's not the way it was.'

Indeed, that's not the way it was at all. He says, 'I had to go training five nights a week and then play a match every Saturday or Sunday. During the week, I wouldn't get home until 9.30pm, too late to play with my friends. They would be going to the cinema or hanging out in the street together and I'd be putting on my kit to train.

'There were times I didn't want to go, I just wanted to give it all up. I wanted to hang with my mates, go to the cinema, just do normal stuff.

'My mum and dad would say to me, "If you want to be a professional footballer, you have to make sacrifices," and then they would put me in the car and drive me to the training ground. I would go to school and then I would go training – that was my life.

'Sometimes I'd say, "I can't be bothered to go training, I don't want to go," but my mum or dad would always be telling me I had to be committed if I wanted to get anywhere. I knew if I didn't do it, I wouldn't become a professional footballer, but it was still hard. I was only a kid and I felt I was missing out on life because I couldn't be with the other lads, couldn't do the things they were doing. I loved my football, really loved it, but at a young age what you most want to do is be one of the gang, hang out with your mates and just kick a ball around in the street.

'But I had to be disciplined to get where I've got now and I've worked hard for it. I do not see myself as a hero, whatever people say or write about me. I've still got a long way to go and, if you believe all the things said about you when you're doing well, you have to look at them when you're not having the same success. You only need one bad game and things change and that can knock your confidence if you let it.'

Wayne's every waking moment was occupied by football and he spent most of his time in the class-room day-dreaming about his heroes rather than concentrating on his work. He admits, 'I look back now and realise I should have given more time to my schoolwork but, when you're a kid, you don't listen to the best advice.

'Mainly, it was football that got me into trouble. I wasn't interested in anything else and just wanted to play all the time. I had a few detentions, too – I spent a lot of time running out of school to the chippie or to have a kick about. Then, if Mum and Dad weren't happy, I was grounded.

'Often, I'd get to school looking smart – black blazer, trousers, tie and white shirt. But, by the time I got home, I often had rips in my trousers. Mum would be upset, and give me a clip because it meant she had to buy me a new pair. She'd never let me go to school with ripped trousers. No way!

'The only subject I liked at school was maths, it's the only GCSE I sat. By then, I was 16 and already knew I had a future at Everton so I couldn't see the point of doing more.'

Wayne's reliance on Coleen shouldn't be under-estimated. He credits her as his soulmate, the person who knows him best and who helps him keep his feet on the ground. He says, 'Coleen won't let me start thinking I am something I'm not, she keeps me where I belong, down to earth. People pay you all these compliments and it's an honour but you could start to believe it if you're not careful.

'Coleen skits me about it. If I've got a bit of a cob on she'll say, "Who do you think you are? Pele?" It's Coleen that really knows me, probably better than anyone else. Our relationship has come a long, long way and there's nothing we don't share.'

Wayne likes to play the clown, even once donning a peroxide-blonde wig Coleen had used when she played Sandy in a school production of *Grease* to take her out. He insisted they go into town – but Coleen knew him too well to let him get away with a wind-up.

While he stood at the bar, sipping a Diet Coke, she popped off to the ladies – then hid behind a post, making it look like he was simply an oddball all on his own.

Says Wayne, 'We have a lot of fun together, we laugh a lot. I can't speak highly enough about her, she's just amazing, my soulmate. She's a special lady.

'She's dead clever, too – much cleverer than me, but, then, I sing better, especially in the bath!'

While Wayne heaps praise on Coleen, she giggles and gives him sideways glances, raising her eyes to the ceiling, especially over his crooner claims.

'He's just a dead bighead,' she says, and dissolves into giggles as he blusters in mock disagreement.

Watching them together was touching. They are each the prop on which the other leans, like two peas from the same pod, sharing a closeness and understanding that comes from a shared background and shared values.

Wayne, surprisingly, was the more talkative of the two but clammed up when Coleen spoke, out of consideration but also a recognition that she may have felt overwhelmed. He watched her like a hawk, discreetly but always with a desire to make sure she was content and to let her know she was the focus of his admiring attention.

Any suggestion that theirs is nothing more than a teen infatuation which will run its course or, worse, run off course due to his celebrity status and the glossy gold-diggers who, inevitably, will throw themselves at his feet appears ill-founded. If anything, Wayne seemed the keener of the two and didn't mind who knew it.

And it's not surprising Wayne is so smitten. Coleen is a really likeable girl, all soft curves and glowing skin, untainted by cynicism and with a vulnerable air which would make anyone want to hug her. Her smile lights her face, showing off beautiful, gleaming-white teeth and the kind of graceful cheekbones a supermodel would envy.

But behind her clear, cat-green eyes there's the tick-tock of a bright, clever mind – Coleen is nobody's fool and, like Wayne, has a stash of life wisdom invested by sound parenting.

She's now an assured member of the Footballer's Wives set, counting among her phone numbers the likes of Victoria Beckham in her little black book, but she's unfazed by the status. She says, 'When I first met the rest of the England wives and girlfriends, I was dead nervous, it's like meeting people you've only ever seen on the telly. But I soon realised they were all just like me. Victoria was lovely, dead down-to-earth, not posh or anything like that – and nobody calls her that either.

'It annoyed me when we got home from Portugal that people were making out she was stand-offish and hadn't been out with the rest of the girls. It just wasn't true, she was out with us all the time. I got on well with Victoria, we exchanged numbers and I've no doubt we'll keep in touch.

'It was nice being with the other girls in Portugal, because we were all going through the same thing. We all agreed that we love our men but miss them like crazy when they're not with us. Me, Victoria, Frank Lampard's partner Ellen, Ian Walker's wife Suzie and John Terry's partner Toni all got on really well. I'm still in touch with them. In fact, the boys said us being so close helped bring them closer together.'

But despite hob-nobbing with the jet-set, Coleen remains an unpretentious, home-loving girl. While Victoria Beckham is famed for her shopping trips to the exclusive Italian fashion capital Milan, splashing out £8,000 on a single outfit, Coleen still trawls the high street or shops at Liverpool's designer store Cricket, run by one of her old schoolfriends. She says, 'I do like designer clothes but that's not a recent thing – my mum and dad used to buy me designer stuff for birthdays and Christmas.

'I love Cricket in Liverpool … I've bought some lovely

dresses from there, but I also go to Zara or Top Shop. I've got an eye for a bargain – I don't like getting ripped off. I think value for money is important. I go shopping with my friends from school – I've still got a close set from my childhood and they often come round to the house for lunch.'

Wayne, of course, enjoys surprising Coleen – he bought her an expensive diamond-and-white-gold ring with his first ever pay after he signed for Everton, saving up until he could afford something 'dead special', and has since lavished her with expensive watches, bracelets and necklaces. The couple have no immediate plans to wed, preferring instead to concentrate on getting their home straight – and taking a breather after the frenzy of Euro 2004. Says Coleen, 'There's no reason for us to get married yet, we can have a long engagement, for as long as we like. We got engaged because we wanted to make a commitment to each other, but it doesn't mean we have to rush off and get married straight away. I liked all the thrones and stuff Victoria had at her wedding, but I want to do something different.

'I love being with Wayne, he's dead caring, he makes me feel special. He cheers me up with his funny sense of humour – he's a great mimic and he's always doing impressions of people off the telly. I know he's the man I want to be with for the rest of my life but we've still got the rest of our lives ahead of us.

'We're still getting used to our life – I still find it hard to believe that my Wayne is the Wayne Rooney who gets his name chanted on the pitch. When he scores, I have to look back and think, That's my

CITY OF LIMERICK PUBLIC LIBRARY

Wayne, the man I love. I can hardly believe it, it doesn't seem real. Afterwards, when I'm on my own and I read about the goals in the newspapers, I get a huge surge of love and pride.

'The thing is, I'm still not great on football – Wayne has tried to teach me about the offside rule but I still don't understand it.'

The couple both love kids – Coleen says they'd like a boy and a girl – but for the moment they are content to lavish their love on her six-year-old sister Rosie.

Rosie suffers from Rett syndrome, a neurological disorder which means she is slowly losing her ability to do everyday tasks, like eating and walking. Wayne recently became the youngster's godfather and says, 'I was dead chuffed to be asked. Rosie has stolen my heart. She's very poorly but always laughing – and Coleen reckons she is always flirting with me. Rosie can't crawl, so I lift her up and put her on the bed and lie next to her, singing nursery rhymes or her favourite songs from The Tweenies.'

Coleen, who also has two brothers – Anthony, 14, and Joe, 16 – said, 'When she comes to our house, it's Wayne she wants, she's dead in love with him – the only rival I've got for his attention.'

Wayne has helped raise many thousands of pounds for Claire House on the Wirral, where Rosie sometimes goes for respite care, and Liverpool's Alder Hey Hospital. The warm-hearted star donated the football boots he scored with against Arsenal to the Rocking Horse Appeal at the hospital.

The boots were auctioned at the appeal's Tiara Ball at

the city's St George's Hall, and attracted widespread attention from supporters of both Everton and Alder Hey. Everton Vice-Chairman Bill Kenwright opened the bidding the day Wayne handed over the boots with a £1,000 pledge and, 24 hours before the event, the appeal received a whopping £5,800 bid. But the auction closed at a staggering £10,000, received from an anonymous Everton supporter, whose cash went towards the £10 million needed to build the first integrated cancer unit for children in the UK.

Madeleine Fletcher from the Appeal says, 'We were all delighted when Wayne chose to give the boots to the Appeal. But we could never have anticipated the incredible excitement generated by the gesture!'

Wayne, who has stunned kids at the hospital by visiting them on his last two birthdays and sharing his birthday cake, also donated the £100,000 to the Appeal raised from his eighteenth-birthday bash, and he later gave the Appeal a further £50,000 earned from a photo shoot with a magazine. He says, 'I wanted to help Claire House because of Rosie, and Alder Hey is where I would have gone if I needed treatment as a kid. It's my local hospital and I wanted to help them. It's people like Rosie and the kids at that hospital who are heroes, not people on the England pitch. They are the ones who deserve all the praise, they are brave and you just don't realise what they have to face every day. It really is amazing how brave these kids are, it's moving. It makes you realise how lucky you are, especially me. It's an honour to be able to give something back to people who will never have the chance to do what I have done.'

One little boy who will never forget Wayne's kindness is seven-year-old Patrick Willers. He was the mascot who held Wayne's hand as they walked out on to the pitch for the fateful England–France game at Euro 2004. The lad had won the once-in-a-lifetime honour after being entered in a McDonald's competition searching for deserving kids.

The football-mad youngster, who lives in Essex with his widowed mum Moira and autistic brother Karl, 11, says, 'Wayne told me not to be nervous and showed me where to stand, because I was in the wrong place. He was whispering so nobody else could hear. I was really proud to hold his hand, I felt great about it. I am a fan of his so I was nervous but he was really nice to me. I support Spurs and Crystal Palace but Wayne is still my favourite player. I think he has brilliant skills – it was so exciting watching the England game against France. I was so close I saw the mud go up when Wayne won his penalty. Now I've got a video of Wayne and I am learning to copy his volley.'

Mum Moira, whose partner died when Patrick was five months old, says, 'He's mad about Wayne, has all the cuttings about him. It was the making of a dream come true for Patrick. His eyes were out on stalks and he hasn't stopped talking about it since.'

But the last words go to Patrick. He says, 'Wayne's brilliant, he's a king on the pitch. I wish him lots and lots of luck and hope he goes to bed early like me so he can get enough sleep to keep scoring goals.'

I knew that time was running out; I thought it was worth me having a go. I saw a gap in the top corner of the goal and just aimed for it. When the ball went in, I couldn't contain MYSELF!

6

YOUNG GUN

IF THERE WAS one match that defined the young Wayne Rooney, it was the one that took place on 19 October 2002, a date which has passed into footballing history. No Everton fan who witnessed that match and Wayne's fantastic début goal will ever forget it. Rueful Arsenal fans might want to try.

This was the day when Wayne's potential was emphatically realised in grand style. He was a sub for much of the match at Goodison and the 40,000-strong crowd were full of anticipation. Few expected the home side to win. After all, they were playing the acknowledged giants of football, Arsenal, who had set a Premiership record of 30 games without defeat, more than seven months without anyone to touch them.

The Gunners had Seaman, Lauren, Campbell, Cygan, Cole, Ljungberg (later substituted by Edu), Gilberto,

Vieira, Touré (who was substituted by Wiltord), Henry and Kanu (who was subbed by Jeffers). David Moyes used the same side he'd deployed when Everton previously played Manchester United, a match which had then ended in defeat. Once again, there was Wright, Hibbert, Yobo, Weir, Unsworth, Carsley (who was substituted by Stubbs), Gravesen, Li Tie (subbed by Linderoth), Pembridge, Campbell and Radzinski, whose substitute was Wayne. The teenager was playing in a Premiership game for only the ninth time.

Contrary to expectations, Everton made the stronger start, as Thomas Gravesen put the pressure on David Seaman from over 30 yards within the first couple of minutes. Tomasz Radzinski followed it up with a powerful shot that went wide. Mark Pembridge's corner was also a near thing for the Gunners' goalie, making him look vulnerable for the first time in the game.

It wasn't long before Arsenal showed their formidable skill. Thierry Henry dashed down the left, beating three players before he made it to Everton's area. Captain David Weir slipped up, allowing Henry to cross to Kanu. David Unsworth should have cleared, but the Everton defence froze and, when Ljungberg thumped home in the eighth minute, it raised still further the widely held expectation that Arsenal would sail through with aplomb. The Frenchman's fine goal had raised their record for goals scored in consecutive matches to 49; this was a case of business as usual. As Liverpool had won against Leeds, it seemed as if Arsenal would soon be back at the top of the league.

Yet Gravesen was determined not to give an inch to

Patrick Vieira and he kept the pressure up until he was able to get past Arsenal to pass to Lee Carsley, who hit a sizzling shot against the post. Just as the attack seemed to have been for nothing, Radzinski, who had been showing tremendous pace throughout the game, was able to pick up the ball on the rebound, dash into the box and, having got past two defenders, send in an angled equaliser for Everton from 15 yards. He almost had another, but was foiled by Lauren at the last second.

Just before half-time, Radzinski gave Ashley Cole cause for alarm, before tumbling in Arsenal's corner as they raced for the ball. Gravesen beat Gilberto Silva before being denied by a decisive save from Seaman.

In the second half, Kolo Touré came close to pulling Arsenal ahead, while Radzinski charged through the Gunners' defence. Lauren retaliated by skimming through Everton's back line, but Henry completely missed a gilt-edged chance and went wide.

Shortly after an hour had elapsed, Sylvain Wiltord was brought on for Touré and hit a real zinger into the post almost immediately. He set up Ljungberg to chip goalie Wright, but, as the ball bounced, it seemed to hit something and, rather than lobbing in, it bent around the outside of the post. Arsenal fans stared down despondently and Wiltord failed to raise their spirits by sending a shot over the crossbar.

Some 20 minutes before the end of the game, Arsenal brought on Francis Jeffers. As might have been predicted, Everton fans were not kind to their former star as he made his appearance. But any ill feeling from the massed ranks of the Toffees was soon to be dispersed.

Having performed magnificently, it was in the eightieth minute that Radzinski made way for Wayne, who'd waited his turn patiently. He gave the crowd a last-minute drama that nobody could have predicted. Like all the best performers, Wayne was saving the best for last.

As soon as he was off his leash, he tore into the opposition relentlessly, demonstrating the self-assurance of a player many years older, making the most of the last minutes of the match. Arsenal's defenders were confounded at every turn by him. He had the ball off Sol Campbell almost at once. Had he done nothing more, it would have been an admirable performance. But there was so much more to come.

Gravesen looped a pass over to Wayne, who showed an instinctive mastery of technique as the ball dropped to him and he weighed up all the options as it zeroed in at a steep angle towards him. He brought it under control with consummate skill, looking as if he had all the time in the world, rather than having to make a split-second decision in front of 40,000 screaming fans and under pressure from some of the world's best defenders. Immediately, he turned and just the most casual of glances told him that David Seaman was vulnerable; from 25 yards, Wayne sent the most cunning of shots veering and dipping towards the goal.

'It was absolutely wonderful – a moment I will never, ever forget,' he later enthused on Everton's website. 'Although I was some distance from the goal, I knew that time was running out; I thought it was worth me having a go. I saw a gap in the top corner of the goal and just aimed for it. When the ball went in, I couldn't contain myself!'

Just ten minutes after he came on, the amazing young talent had the ball sailing over the mighty David Seaman. His left hand at full stretch, the goalie couldn't quite reach the ball, which went crashing into the roof of the net from under the bar, leaving the 39-year-old floundering in the wake of Wayne's outstanding drive.

Suddenly seeming very much his age, the veteran goalkeeper could do nothing but trudge sadly to the back of the net to retrieve the ball. There had been moments in the match when he was more than equal to serious challenges. In the second half, Gravesen had aimed a powerful shot at the bottom corner, only to see Seaman's palm appear to frustrate his efforts. What had gone wrong at this late stage for Arsenal?

Some critics may have been quick to plant the blame squarely in the hands of the ageing goalkeeper, who had already let in an inswinging corner against Macedonia earlier in the week. And, despite the warm cheers from both sides which had greeted the England veteran when he ran on to the pitch, everyone knew he couldn't go on for ever. He was, literally, old enough to be Wayne's father. In past years, ran one train of thought, he would have been quicker and sharper and would surely never have let the goal through. The harsher view was that he was just open to attack from a long range. Yet Chris Woods, the Everton goalkeeping coach, whose 43 international caps put him almost on a level with Seaman, had no doubt about the truth of the amazing goal that clinched the match. He accompanied Seaman off the pitch, an arm around his colleague's shoulder, as they walked into the tunnel. 'If there had been three 'keepers on the line, I doubt whether they could have done anything about Wayne's goal,' Woods later said. 'No 'keeper on earth would have kept that out. As an example of individual brilliance, it was out of this world.'

The reality began to sink in. Seaman's performance couldn't have been better. It was simply that the Gunners could do nothing against Wayne's unstoppable onslaught. Edu claimed that he should have been awarded a penalty in the dying seconds of the match. But there was no way out, despite an extra period of time, announced as being two minutes but actually lasting for a nerve-shredding five minutes in total. For both sets of supporters, it seemed as if the final whistle would never come.

When it did, Everton fans went absolutely mad. They simply didn't want to go home! Nobody could quite believe what they'd seen and they wanted to make the most of it and who could blame them? As the team jubilantly left the pitch and reached the sanctuary of the dressing rooms, they could hear the crowd still cheering outside. The players added their voices to the celebrations, leaping around and Wayne was at the centre of the excitement.

Outside, the loudest cheers of all came from Wayne's family. After the match, proud father Wayne Sr gave the teenager a big hug, summing up better than any words how the Rooneys felt. Jeanette was so overcome with emotion that she burst into floods of tears. Wayne later said that he thought that she was more affected by the occasion that even he was! It was the combination of her son's big moment and the turnaround in fortunes for their beloved club.

But, for different reasons, hers weren't the only tears of the evening. The shock defeat left Arsenal stunned and their fans numb with shock. This was no ordinary result. It's not far from the truth to say that the London side had forgotten what it was like to be losers. This was the first time that the Gunners had been defeated since 18 December 2001, when they lost to Newcastle. That Liverpool victory over Leeds now meant they were no longer top of the league. And it was all down to that young powerhouse who was the newest of new recruits to the Premiership and who had taken just ten minutes to remind everyone just what football is all about. What a way for Wayne to begin his career!

Nothing quite like it had ever been seen in football. It was hard to fathom that, just one season earlier, Wayne was only a reserve player. In every way, Wayne's début was assured and powerful. Not content with putting a stop to the unbeaten record set by Arsenal, his goal also set one of his own, the first of many. Just five days short of his seventeenth birthday, he became the youngest player to score in the Premiership.

David Moyes knew that too much praise could be overwhelming for his young star, but couldn't help enthusing, 'It was a wonderful goal, a wonderful finish. There are special players who have graced the game down the years and Wayne can go on to become another.'

With good humour, he added, 'But I won't let him get carried away – he hasn't scored all week in training.'

Moyes revealed that that speculative shot from 25 yards that had been executed so perfectly was something Wayne had been told off for doing at Everton. 'Sometimes we have a bit of a go at him for trying unrealistic shots from that range,' he explained, 'but this time I felt with the space in front of him that he had a serious chance to score and he did it pretty well.'

It was safe to assume that he wasn't going to be given a dressing-down for his efforts that Saturday. There was no doubting the special place that Wayne held for the manager, who explained that, despite the scale of Wayne's success, 'The encouraging thing is that his feet are on the ground. He'll probably celebrate by going out with his pals. He's like that, level-headed.'

And Wayne himself knew that, even with such a natural talent, he still had work to do. 'The most important thing is that I continue to listen to the manager, the coaches and to my team-mates,' he said in the days following the win. 'I must try and improve as a player each and every day.'

There were no sour grapes from the side whose celebrated 'va va voom' seemed to be a little lacking. In fact, the opposite was true. Arsenal manager Arsène Wenger was unstinting in his praise of the lad who had wrecked his team's reputation with one kick.

'To lose our record is a big disappointment, but at least we lost to a special goal from a special talent. Seaman had no chance with their winner. There is no goalkeeper in the world who would have stopped that goal,' admitted Wenger. 'He's the biggest English talent I've seen since I took over at Highbury. He is supposed to be 16, but I didn't know that 16-year-olds could do things like that. He is everything you could dream of – intelligence, quick reactions, strong running with the ball.'

It was undeniable and the experienced manager gave an accurate prediction of things to come. 'He has huge potential. He's more than just a goalscorer. He is not the guy who just stands in the box and waits to score. You can put him on the wing, you can put him in the centre, you can put him behind the striker. He can play people in and dribble – I like strikers who can do that – and he's a clever, natural footballer. He's special, all right. The guy can play.'

Even a remarkably astute young man such as Wayne probably didn't quite expect the seismic reaction to his earth-shattering performance. But, in the fast-moving world of football, stunned disbelief was followed by amazement as even the hard-bitten sport correspondents had to sit up and take notice. 'THE BOY WONDER' ran a headline in the *Daily Mail*. Even the sober *Times* was forced to acknowledge, 'ROONEY GRABS THE LIMELIGHT'. Bookies William Hill were reported to be offering odds of 7–2 that Wayne would become England's youngest international player. As it turned out, anyone who took them up on the offer would be laughing all the way to the pay-out window!

In the rush to try and put a recognisable name to this seeming force of nature, there were few great players that Wayne wasn't compared to. Michael Owen was an obvious equivalent, not least because he held the record as the youngest Premiership goalscorer before Wayne. The Liverpool player was 17 years and 145 days old when he first scored, though that was practically ready to qualify for his OAP bus pass in comparison to Wayne! And it wasn't just in age that he dazzled.

'I didn't see Owen as a 16-year-old,' said Arsène Wenger, 'but I'd call him a complete striker. Rooney, on the other hand, already looks to be a complete footballer. He is strongly built with a low centre of gravity, a bit like Paul Gascoigne. I've seen Rooney come off the bench a few times, most recently against Manchester United, and you don't have to be a connoisseur to see he's out of the ordinary.'

For David Moyes, there was another comparison. 'I thought Charlie Nicholas was the best 16-year-old I ever saw. But Rooney is better than Charlie was at that age. If things go well, if we do the right things, we could have a player. Wayne has tremendous ability and, the most precious thing of all, a real football intelligence.'

Amid the excitement and celebration, there were voices which sounded a note of caution, wondering if Wayne would stay with Everton or if such talent would inevitably be tempted elsewhere. David Moyes moved quickly to dispel any rumblings, however distant. 'If I want to keep players, then the board will always support me, no matter what the offer is. I want to lay foundations that will not be knocked away,' he insisted. 'Why should Everton not be trying to compete with Manchester United and Arsenal? It would be an insult to fans to say that we should sell our best players.'

Others were concerned that the youngster's ability could be burned out, the familiar, tragic scenario acted out by all too many young princes of football. Manchester United's Sir Alex Ferguson said, 'He looks so mature and strong. I've heard David Moyes wants to handle him like we did Ryan Giggs and keep him out of the spotlight and that's a good idea.'

This was exactly Moyes's plan. 'He still has a lot of developing to do,' said the manager. 'He's still just a young boy who is happy with a ball at his feet. At that age, the last thing you want is to expose them to even more publicity and I'll bring Wayne along as carefully as I can.'

Former Everton manager Walter Smith was upbeat. 'The football world's full of so-called superkids who were burned out before they became 20,' he observed. 'I'm as sure as I can be that won't happen with Wayne. He has a really good attitude, he's a very down-to-earth boy. I'm certain, with the help of Davie Moyes and the staff at Everton, he'll be all right. The boy's sensible and so are his parents. Naturally, I've met them and that's why I don't have any fears for him.'

Smith, who was also manager at Rangers, had watched Wayne develop at Everton in the Academy and was well aware of his all-round impressiveness. 'There is justification for getting excited about this boy. He doesn't rely on one aspect of the game – not sheer pace, goalscoring instinct, passing ability, or dribbling to take on defenders. People who hadn't seen him before Saturday wonder when you talk about his abilities, but he's got them in abundance.'

If there were any further proof required of Wayne's shattering power, it was found in Arsenal's poor performance the following Tuesday. It was a Champions League match against Auxerre that should have been a walkover, but the former all-conquering warriors suddenly looked nervous, indecisive and shadows of their former selves.

And who could blame them? Nobody likes to be reminded of their own weaknesses and Arsenal were no exception. He might not have been anywhere near the pitch, but the presence of a certain Evertonian teenager pervaded the match as Arsenal suffered a surprise 2–1 defeat against the French side, though they eventually made it to the second stage of the competition.

'You have to give credit to Auxerre for the way they played,' said Arsène Wenger, before going on to admit the real source of his side's lacklustre performance. 'But I don't think my team had fully recovered from the shock of losing on Saturday and we looked fatigued in the first half.'

Even Guy Roux, the manager of Auxerre, made what some thought to be a coded reference to the new Everton star when he commented on the match. 'When you imagine how Arsenal can play, this was different. The balls to feet and the continental style were both missing, and that was a bit of a surprise for us.'

It was a bit of a surprise to everyone who saw it. Wayne's first Premiership goal had been a wake-up call to everyone in football and the reverberations would be heard around the world. He had a way to go before he became the superstar who strode out to battle during

Euro 2004, but there was a fireball of excitement which had begun after that goal and would spread out to encompass even those who had only the most casual interest in football. His name would be everywhere. And it was in the last few minutes of that match against Arsenal that it all really began for Wayne Rooney.

His life would never be the same again, but this was no overnight success. This was the target that Wayne had worked hard to hit since the first time he blasted holes in the paintwork on his nan's wall.

I'VE Ive always dreamed of signing for Everton and I always knew it would **HAPPEN.**

7

SUB STANDARDS

THE JOURNEY TO football stardom began almost as soon as Wayne was old enough to kick a ball. But, however good he was and however often he played, it wasn't until he actually started training with his beloved Everton that he could really stand up and say that his most cherished dreams were becoming a reality.

Life as an apprentice footballer was that much more demanding than kicking a ball around with friends or starring in the local leagues. After Everton scout Bob Pendleton spotted Wayne playing in the Copplehouse team for the Under-10s, the boy wowed the Walton and Kirkdale Junior Football League with those staggering 99 goals in his final season. Everton snapped him up and he joined the Blues Academy where he immediately set about shattering records – something that was to become a bit of a pattern for him in his footballing career. In his first season playing in the Liverpool Schools FA Under-11s, he knocked out a record 72 goals and went on to do so well in his training that he could have skipped much of it.

Colin Harvey was the Under-19s coach. A devoted Evertonian, he had a bittersweet tenure as manager in the early 1990s, but he showed great sensitivity and skill in the way he brought on Wayne Rooney. He realised that the boy was ready to join his squad by the turn of the century, when he was just 14. Wayne repaid that faith by scoring his first goal for him the following year.

As Wayne started to transform his lifelong dedication to Everton from fervent supporter to personal contributor, his team's fortunes were fluctuating. The last few years had been tough for Everton, but they hung on.

Their survival instinct is a trait which has always been part of the team's make-up. Their fans are proud to be part of a side who were one of the founding members of the football league back in 1888 and whose story has been one of determination and dedication – mirroring Wayne's own rise to prominence.

From its earliest days as the St Domingo School team in the 1870s, when the players would set up the goalposts themselves on the first pitch, then in Stanley Park, the team quickly earned a reputation. By 1879, they had decided to call themselves Everton FC. It wasn't until the turn of the century that they settled on the distinctive blue strip that Wayne was so proud to wear.

Their base was moved several times before they settled on Mere Green Field. They set about transforming the site into the pitch that Wayne grew up to know and cherish as much as his family home, Goodison Park. It was opened in the summer of 1892. It was only a few years into the twentieth century before the team were able to congratulate themselves on being FA Cup winners on two occasions.

Between the war years, Everton fans were taken on a roller-coaster ride of highs and lows as they finished top of the league in the 1927/28 season. But then disaster struck just two seasons later as they crashed and were relegated to the Second Division. Hearts still in mouths, the team regained their pole position in the First Division in 1931/32 and topped that by lifting the FA Cup in 1933. They shone again in the last years of the 1930s, but the post-war line-ups of much of the 1950s were nothing for a promising player like Wayne to look back on.

As England woke up to the Swinging Sixties, Everton returned to form, coming top of the First Division in the 1963/64 season. In the middle of the 1960s, such a glorious decade for English football, the Toffees seized the FA Cup for the third time, some 33 years after their previous win. They won the Championship again at the end of the decade, showing themselves to be every inch the team that Wayne was to be so proud of.

If the 1970s were not nearly as spectacular, the 1980s were once again a golden period for this most resilient of clubs. They fought back from deepest mediocrity to win the FA Cup once more in the 1983/84 season and they followed that up in the following year by sailing to both European and League titles.

They kept up a more than respectable level of success in the last years of the decade, but there were few causes for celebration in the early 1990s. It did nothing to shake Wayne's faith in his side and showed just how dedicated the young boy was to the team into which he'd been born, as they were almost relegated in 1994. But they fought back to win the FA Cup again in the following year, perhaps the least-fancied side to do so.

The latter years of the 1990s and the years leading up to Wayne's début were decidedly mixed, with Everton seemingly unable to do more than fight fire for much of the time. Everton's recent history was a dramatic illustration of how welcome was the injection of Wayne's talent.

In any year, any club would have been delighted to have someone of his epoch-making abilities on their side, but it came at a particularly opportune time for the Toffees. After a century of football marked by fleeting flashes of pure genius, Everton once more had a home-grown talent of colossal stature.

As Wayne set out on his career proper with Everton in 2002, he was able to draw inspiration from a host of outstanding players from the club's illustrious past. One of the earliest heroes was Fred Geary, who scored 86 times in 96 appearances at the club around the turn of the century.

Still revered was the outstanding centre-forward Dixie Dean. Idolised by Everton fans, he stood in the line of truly awesome players at the end of which is

Wayne himself. Between 1927 and 1928, he scored a record 60 goals in 39 league matches.

After he left the club in 1937, his crown was seized by Tommy Lawton, a worthy successor who, aged 18, became the youngest player to score for Everton. No prizes for guessing who would shatter that record! Lawton's performance lifted the club's spirits before his triumphant reign was cruelly cut short by World War II in 1940.

In more recent times, there have been other names which must have been powerful encouragement for a football-mad youngster such as Wayne. Gary Lineker enjoyed a personally successful, if brief, run at the club following their amazing 1984/85 season. But now there was a new name to add to the roster of greats.

There were already hints of the glory to come as Wayne moved up through the Academy. Former Everton boss Walter Smith saw him play on many weekends, but the boy was too young to play in the first team. 'Not only would I like to have had him in my team, so would every football manager of every club in the country,' says Smith. 'I would have loved to have thrown him on and I was very tempted, especially when we had all our main attackers out injured.'

Wayne signed up to be an Everton scholar in December 2001, when he was presented to the fans at a packed ceremony in Goodison Park in front of then-chairman Sir Philip Carter. Ray Hall, director of the Academy, spoke for the entire club when he exclaimed, 'Everyone at the club is delighted that Wayne has decided to sign for us. Hopefully, there will be many successful years ahead for both the player and the club.'

Wayne's majestic performance in the FA Youth Cup of 2002 was a foretaste of the form he would show in the opening years of his professional career. He had already made an appearance, albeit on the benches, for the Premiership match against Southampton on 20 April. Disappointingly for the youngster, David Moyes didn't call on him and he could only watch as his side cruised to a 1–0 victory with a powerful display. It only served to make Wayne even more determined to impress in the struggle for the Youth Cup.

There was already much to be proud of – he had only left school the Friday before his great turn against Spurs in the semis, when he first showed David Moyes his aptitude for scoring from long range. When the Everton team faced Villa in the final that May, the Cup might not have eventually come home to Goodison Park, but Wayne was still named Player of the Final.

The following month, donning his England Under-17s team shirt, he shone once again when he proved to be a key part of taking England to third place in the Championships. A hat-trick in the playoffs for third and fourth place against Spain took his personal score to five goals in five games and an enviable total of eight goals in the Cup.

By now, it was inevitable that Wayne would be a crucial part of any Everton side. The passionate young man was not yet 17, but his focus and drive meant that his early début in the Premiership was assured.

So it was that he played his first game in the big time on 17 August in a match against Spurs. In some ways, it wasn't the occasion it could have been. Wayne looked so at home in the Premiership match that anyone would have thought he'd been playing in games at that level for years. What that furrowed brow hid as he went out on the pitch was his real sense of amazement. I was just another face in the crowd last year, he thought to himself, now I'm going to be out there!

Watched by some of his former heroes, including Bob Latchford and Alex Young, Wayne played for 66 minutes and acquitted himself well, beginning a rise to prominence which was nothing short of earth-shattering.

Everton fans quickly took Wayne to their hearts. He was the boy who had gone all the way, who showed all true Blues that it was possible to live the dream and go from being a fan to a local hero to playing at the highest levels. Here was the youngster who was open about admitting his passion. 'I honestly cannot find the words to describe the feeling I get when I run out at Goodison Park wearing that famous blue shirt,' he says.

However well he might do in his career, Wayne would always hold a special place at Everton. And he was never conceited about his success. 'I knew the night before that I'd be playing,' he says of that first big game. 'I just went home, watched a few videos and played some computer games before going to bed.' No wonder many called him a people's player!

A little under a month later, Wayne received his first yellow card in a match against Middlesbrough. The Toffees won 2–1, but Wayne was unable to turn his scoring opportunities into goals, even though his performance notably livened up the match. Apart from the yellow card, which arose from an incident with Mark Schwarzer, Wayne – who replaced Niclas Alexandersson in the second half – was already beginning to make a charismatic contribution to Everton's games. He had a strength and aggressive edge to his striking technique that was marking him out as a uniquely gifted player.

In total, Wayne would be booked eight times and sent off once in Everton's season. But this was nothing more than a reflection of the ruthlessness that any striker has to show if they are to make an impact. Manchester United legend Norman Whiteside insisted that Wayne had nothing to worry about.

'Rooney is the type of player who's going to find himself in trouble with referees at times because he's got that nasty streak, which top players need,' explained Whiteside. 'He's got that little bit of edge.' He was also still at that age when he was easy to provoke, something which challenging players soon latched on to and used to their advantage.

It wasn't long before Wayne showed how much more he was capable of. On 1 October, he was named on the bench against Wrexham in the opening round of the Worthington Cup. After 64 minutes, Wayne was subbed for Tomasz Radzinski. He strode out from the benches, tense but ready to repay all that faith placed in him.

Wayne bided his time, his set face showing the incredible will power which had brought him so far. In the 83rd minute, the ball was flicked to him from the great Duncan Ferguson in a clearance from Richard Wright. The defence had no chance as Wayne barrelled past to score his first goal. He followed that up just before the end of normal time and was a whisker away from a hat-trick, denied by the closest of saves.

That day, Wayne broke the record for the youngest ever goalscorer at Everton, held for more than 60 years by Tommy Lawton. With his first goals, Wayne had already won himself a place in the Everton history books! Team-mate Ferguson, who has himself often been the centre of hero-worship at Everton, knew how the fans would feel. 'They're very proud of him and quite rightly so. Wayne's a Scouser so he's one of them and it's great for the supporters,' said the Scot. 'It's great for Everton, too, that one of their strikers is leading the line for England.'

By the autumn of 2002, it was said that David Moyes had vowed to quit the club if Rooney was sold to pay off club debts and there were few who would say that his determination was misplaced. Wayne was due to sign his first professional contract with Everton in the week that he scored his triumphant and unforgettable début goal against Arsenal. With a pay rise that anyone would be glad to receive, it saw his £80 per week apprentice wages soar to £8,000 – or it would have done if it had gone ahead. It was announced that there would be a delay.

As was only to be expected in a club as close-knit as Everton, one not unused to seeing their best-loved players disappear at inopportune moments, rumours began to circulate. They'd seen it happen before, most infamously to the hugely popular Duncan Ferguson, but they also had to endure Francis Jeffers going to Arsenal and Michael Ball to Rangers. There were so many more reasons for Wayne Rooney to go to another club.

'I will sign my contract with Everton as soon as is possible,' commented Wayne. 'There will be a delay, which is unfortunate. The problem is that my current agent has not agreed to terminate our agreement even though it does run out in December.' Nevertheless, the rumblings continued for the rest of the year. In the meantime, as Wayne's career continued its seemingly unstoppable acceleration into jet-propelled overdrive, there was more to delight the Toffees.

Seeming unaffected by his new-found status, Wayne remained refreshingly down-to-earth. He said, 'I am really enjoying my football at the moment and I love training with the rest of the lads. Even so, I do manage to keep in touch with all my old mates from the youth side, so I don't think I am going to change too much.'

Even so, David Moyes meant every word when he said he was determined not to overexpose Wayne at such an early stage in his development. He left him on the subs bench on Sunday, 27 October when the Blues played West Ham and waited until more than an hour had elapsed before sending him on to replace Radzinski. Many would have bet substantial sums that Wayne would be the first to score but, although he stormed in to take Kevin Campbell's pass, his shot went over. The only goal of the match was in the end scored by Carsley.

Sticking to his tactics, Moyes was not forthcoming on the subject of his wonderkid player after the match. But a big hurdle had been overcome. The team had moved on from the hysteria following the Arsenal win with assurance.

'The players showed a really good performance,' he said, adding with some understatement, 'because maybe there were a few more eyes on us than there were last week.'

The following Sunday, against Leeds, Wayne was again a substitute, coming on in the last quarter of the game to turn Everton's fortunes around. He was mastering the art of being the ticking timebomb, sitting out on the benches until he exploded into action with devastating results, just as he had done against Arsenal.

Even the least superstitious of fans was beginning to despair of victory against Leeds at Elland Road. They had a point – the team hadn't won there for 51 years.

They started well. Leeds had no more than a handful of chances and, aside from a heart-stopping moment courtesy of Jonathan Woodgate, Everton were looking the better side. Leeds goalie Paul Robinson had to deal with a number of valiant early efforts by Everton, including a free kick by Mark Pembridge. Just before half-time, he twice halted Radzinski and then Carsley.

Leeds had to content themselves with penalty appeals, one from Alan Smith after just under half-an-hour had elapsed and another by Nick Barmby shortly afterwards. Barmby received a yellow card for diving, in a disappointing end to the first half for Leeds.

The home team returned to make more headway, but soon lost the initiative to Everton and Robinson once again had to fight off Radzinski with two impressive saves. The Toffees were looking good, but it was still a goal-free match. And, once that Woodgate header had been cleared, Radzinski made way for Wayne Rooney.

David Moyes must have been itching to play his ace card earlier. But he was too wise for that, too determined to nurture his new talent and played it poker-faced. When he felt the time was right, his expression was that of any crack card player – read 'em and weep! On came Wayne Rooney.

The young hero was making quite an art of impressive entrances. In the eightieth minute, Leeds' Lucas Radebe could do little but watch as Wayne kicked a sharply angled shot between his legs and Robinson suddenly appeared helpless before Wayne's thunderous charge. It was a superb run, topped by a low, right-footed shot from inside the box.

It wasn't the 30-yard slammer that wowed everyone at Arsenal, rather a centre-forward's goal, but nobody cared at all. That was all Everton needed, 1–0, and, behind the Leeds goal, the Evertonians leaped from their feet to punch the air and celebrate Wayne's brilliance with a mighty roar. He dashed over to them and jumped high above the Leeds' turf to acknowledge their excitement. He was clearly as proud as they were.

Though the goal against Arsenal had certainly been the more important for Wayne as a player, for the legion of devoted admirers at Everton, it meant the world that he'd broken the spell at Leeds.

The last few months of 2002 were a blur of excitement and success for Wayne and it was little surprise to anyone who took even the slightest interest in his jet-propelled progress that he won the coveted BBC Young

Sports Personality of the Year award. Wayne was the boy that few had heard of outside the world of Everton before his outstanding opening performances in the Premiership. Now everyone was talking about him.

Who else could it have gone to? Well, as it turned out, the competition was tough and, in any other year, it might have gone to either of the runners-up. Charlotte Kerwood was England's youngest medal-winner, with a gold in the women's double-trap at the Commonwealth Games. Becky Owen won silver medals in the gymnastic events at the same games. In the end, though, it was Wayne whose performance impressed the most and Sven-Göran Eriksson was there to hand the lad his well-deserved award.

Sir Bobby Robson was among many who lined up to shower Wayne with praise. 'He's a jewel in the crown,' said the Newcastle boss. It wasn't all applause, as Wayne discovered how hard it can be to live up to people's expectations when the television cameras are on. Outraged viewers telephoned the BBC to report a terrible crime perpetrated by the new star.

It transpired that Wayne had committed the dreadful sin of not only wearing his tie slightly loosened but also … chewing gum! Suddenly, all that footballing ability was forgotten, as Wayne's youthful exuberance was misinterpreted as if it were a deliberate snub. The Beeb were having none of it.

'We did get some complaints,' admitted a spokeswoman, 'but no one connected with the show was the least bit concerned. Everyone thought he was a lovely lad.' To his fans, it showed him to be nothing more than what he was – a teenager, just like any other, displaying all the awkwardness that they often do when they have to dress up smart for an occasion. For someone still on the basic wage of a novice, Wayne was having to grow up far faster than most lads his age.

'Appearing on live television would scare the living daylights out of many a seasoned performer,' stormed a spokesman for Everton later, 'let alone a teenager from Croxteth. The whole thing is preposterous and has been blown out of all proportion.'

Wayne showed the award had been no fluke when he put in another staggering performance against Blackburn just a few days later. Everton were behind following a an early goal by Blackburn's Andy Cole and, in a game during which Rovers played the best football, it was Wayne who shone the brightest.

When one of his shots rebounded off the post, Carsley equalised before Wayne took Everton ahead with a fantastic strike, all before half-an-hour of the match had elapsed. As he took a long clearance from Wright and danced through the Rovers' defence to clip the ball home, many thought of that first amazing goal against Arsenal earlier in the season. This truly was the Young Sports Personality of 2002 at work.

In the second half of the game, Wayne continued to dazzle with long bursts across the pitch to find his colleague Carsley and, despite the club's best efforts to underline the team effort, it was obvious who was on show.

'It's not the Wayne Rooney show,' insisted David Moyes, 'but we're aware of how important he is to us.

He's got all the attributes but, more importantly, he's got football intelligence.'

As if to underline the long-term commitment, Wayne signed a new deal with Everton in January 2003 for three-and-a-half years. This was the maximum time for a player under 18. It was just the boost that Everton fans needed. They all breathed a sigh of relief. This time their fears had been groundless, though the hype around Wayne meant that such stories would always be around.

'I have been an Everton fan all my life,' declared Wayne. 'I never even thought about signing for another club, despite everything that has been written about me in the newspapers recently. I always knew I was going to sign. I've always dreamed of signing for Everton and I always knew it would happen.'

The real reason for the delay was, as Wayne had insisted in October, relatively mundane. Negotiations had taken longer than anyone had anticipated and Wayne changed representation. He was no longer with Peter McIntosh of X8 Sports Management, the company which specialised in developing local talent. They had to sit back and watch as he signed up with Paul Stretford of the Proactive Sports Group before renewing his loyalty to Everton.

The two sides had been sweating over issues to do with image rights, among other business questions. In every way, it was a different league, though officially he would still be a novice when the three years were up. The new deal pushed Wayne's wages from his apprenticeship level of around £80–£90 a week up to a rather more comfortable £13,000 weekly salary. That is quite an apprenticeship!

Speaking in the *Star*, the Blues' boss was clearly ecstatic. 'Give us a bit of time to develop him and England should have a future star in the making. It breaks my heart as a Scotsman to say that, but it's a fact.'

If negotiations over a new contract had provoked debate about Wayne's future with the club, each successive appearance on the pitch – whether for Everton or at international level – caused fresh speculation. It was the story that wouldn't go away.

But David Moyes was determined to guard Wayne as much as he could. Some felt that he could be overprotective at times, particularly when the lad's fitness was in question. During the final game of the season on 11 May 2003, when Everton played at home against Manchester United, they went down 2–1 against the visitors. Not only did that demolish their hopes of winning a place in the UEFA Cup, but Wayne also received a knee injury, despite a strong game in which he created a number of good chances.

Moyes was insistent that this meant he would have to miss out on the chance to travel with the England squad to South Africa. Above all, following such a stressful season, he needed time to rest. But Sven-Göran Eriksson was not convinced. 'Why should he not go to South Africa?' questioned Eriksson. 'I haven't picked the squad yet. But, if he is picked, he will play. Why not?' There were tense conversations between the managers and the conflict was only resolved when the young striker joined the England squad a while later for training in Spain. Moyes's determination to cosset Wayne was totally understandable in terms of the amazing talent he could see developing.

By the end of the first season, Wayne's life had been completely transformed, both on and off the pitch. His personal life was open to scrutiny, but on a practical level it made his job that much more complicated. Whenever he arrived for training he would have to sign autographs and chat with fans. Sometimes, Wayne wished he could just be another kid, anonymous and carefree, but he never showed it, always smiling and joking with those who'd come to catch a glimpse of him.

Stories about Wayne's future continued to flood the press. 'We won't get a single phone call this summer enquiring about Wayne. It's a sign that we are going forward as a club,' said Bill Kenwright. 'Wayne loves Everton and there is no way that he wants to leave us.' If there was any downside to the success at all, it was that Wayne missed being out there with the supporters, singing with the crowd. He was still at heart just a big fan!

In the light of his reputation as being headstrong, some felt he should be warned over getting too heavy on the pitch. Former England captain Terry Butcher saw him as being too eager sometimes. 'Wayne is trying to stamp his mark on senior football and sometimes you can be too impetuous,' he explained. 'But Wayne's aggression is not necessarily a bad fault. That's just youthful naïveté and exuberance. Sometimes you can just get carried away.' These were minor considerations in comparison with the immense contributions the teenager – then widely and affectionately known at Goodison Park as 'Roonaldo' – had made to Everton and the Premiership as a whole in such a short space of time.

The highs of Wayne's first season as a senior were marred as preparations for the new term began. First of all, he got in his manager's bad books by coming back a little wider around the waistline than before – about a stone's worth, to be more exact. Pictures of Wayne snapped by the press on a beach displaying more of his additional cuddliness did nothing to help the situation.

There was a more serious problem to come. Wayne played in a friendly match over the summer against Rangers, which Everton eventually won 3–2. As everyone expected, Wayne started well, ably assisting Radzinski, though the assault came to nothing.

Later in the match came a heavy challenge from defender Robert Malcolm. Wayne crashed to the ground in a heart-stopping moment for the Everton supporters, full of concern for their wonderkid. Their worst fears seemed to be confirmed as Wayne was stretchered off the pitch.

Fortunately, X-rays showed there wasn't a break in the metatarsal bone, though an MRI scan revealed ligament damage. The club and fans sighed with relief as they realised how much worse it could have been. Even so, Wayne was forced to miss the opening of his second season.

For someone as devoted to his craft as Wayne, the enforced absence was torture. Yet he ensured it was as brief as possible and came back in grand style in the match against Charlton Athletic.

This first Premiership clash of the new season made 26 August 2003 a date to remember. Wayne knew he had to perform well not only for his manager but also for the man who would be deciding whether or not he spent the early part of the summer of 2004 in Portugal.

If Sven-Göran Eriksson had any concerns about the fitness of his youngest talent, they were banished by the end of the match. Charlton took the lead with Jason Euell scoring with a penalty. It wasn't to last. Minutes later, Steve Watson equalised.

But again Charlton took the lead with another penalty taken by Euell just after half-time. Wayne was feeling more confident and began to make his presence felt, setting up a chance for Gary Naysmith an hour into the match.

It was up to Wayne himself to secure the equaliser, as Naysmith returned his favour, setting him up with a cross that Wayne controlled with his right foot. He swept the ball off his other foot with a powerful stroke from around ten yards, leaving Dean Kiely flummoxed. Everton kept the pressure up for the rest of the match – a promising start to a season that would be disappointing for the club by comparison with 2002/03. Mere survival was hardly the loftiest of ambitions for the fans for this new season and it was also often frustrating for Wayne. He wasn't on the pitch as much as he'd have liked, and he was having to do his growing up in public, as every game was reported in the media as another outing for the Wayne Rooney Club.

Though the lad was making fantastic progress in his career, at times the pressure of his new-found success showed both in Wayne and in Everton. There was so much attention on him off the pitch that sometimes the distractions spilled over into his beloved game. The eighteenth-birthday bash in October had been a great way to celebrate his coming of age, with so many stars coming out to wish him well, but it hadn't gone down well with his cautious manager.

Moyes would have preferred the extent of his protégé's contact with the media to have been limited to the rare interview he allowed the press with the birthday boy. There, Wayne had said, 'I never thought I would achieve what I have. But I'm always looking to improve and hopefully I will keep going. I just want to do as well as I can for Everton and win a place in Europe – and, hopefully, win Euro 2004 with England.

'I think in some games I have done all right but in others maybe not quite as well.' With commendable honesty, he went on, 'Once I know the game and the players better, I'm sure I can improve. I'm still young and have a lot to learn but, when I play, I know the sort of things I can do better.'

But as the Blues' season sank to a low in November 2003, with the club among the bottom three, the tension was very evident between David Moyes and Wayne.

It boiled over during a match against Bolton on the last Saturday in November. As Moyes himself admitted, nobody in the Everton camp was showing much hunger for victory. The home side never gave Moyes's boys a look-in throughout the first half and the only surprise by half-time was that they weren't more than one goal up.

None of the players was shining, Wayne included. He was slightly hurt when he clashed with goalie Jussi Jaaskelainen and his later attempt to chip one past him went over the crossbar. Before an hour had elapsed, Wayne was subbed for Francis Jeffers and Everton ended up losing 2–0.

As the star left the pitch, he betrayed his youth with a bad-tempered display towards David Moyes. His aggressive playing style was already well known in the game (in total he would be booked 12 times in the season), but this wasn't just a strop at being taken off. As he'd said in his birthday round of interviews, 'It's a bit disappointing when you're not in all the time. But, if the other lads are in the side and doing their job, you have to accept it – it's the manager's decision. As soon as I score a few more goals, I think all the confidence will come back. I've not really played a lot in the last few games and I'm sure it will return.'

The other factor that had come up that week was that he'd flown out to shoot a Coca-Cola commercial in Spain and, although it was with the permission of the club, it was clearly not exactly with his manager's blessing.

'The decision was taken to let him go,' admitted Moyes. 'That has nothing to do with the game, but obviously we want our players to rest when they don't have a game.' In after-match interviews, Moyes was determined to keep the lid on publicity, but it was a continuous struggle. 'I don't want to say too much about Wayne, if you don't mind,' he said. 'I will say he is a young boy who is still young enough to play for the Everton youth team if we wanted him to play in the FA Youth Cup. Let's remember what we are all expecting of him. We have to be careful and I will continue to be careful with his progress.'

He had a point. Amid all the hysteria about England prospects, the licensing deals and the merchandising of his image, it was easy to forget that, at club level, Wayne had by then scored only twice in seven months. His first goal of the season at Goodison Park wasn't to come until December's game against Leicester.

'People at no time have thought of anything but him being a fantastic footballer, rather than the age he is,' said Moyes. 'Senior players get dips in form and sometimes that is even more obvious. At times, it's been difficult but I would not swap it for the world and I wish I had 10, 12 or 14 others like that.' And so said every other manager in the country.

As the months passed, the buzz was no longer about how the star might get the side out of its sizeable pickle, or even if he would stay at Everton, but rather, when he would go. Despite the best efforts by the club, the stories about his imminent departure had never, in truth, gone away and they were redoubled after his amazing performances for England in the run-up to the summer contest.

And yet Wayne was still able to show that he hadn't forgotten about his primary duty to the club which had nursed him from the start. Just weeks before he was due to fly to Portugal, he lent his unmistakeable magic to the 13 March game against Portsmouth. In a side that often seemed to be struggling, he made his move with just under a quarter-of-an-hour of the match to go. Taking the ball from Tomasz Radzinski, he beat John Curtis to unleash one of his trademark bullets past the Pompey goalie, the only goal of the match. As Wayne sped down the pitch to celebrate in front of the visiting fans, stunned Portsmouth were left to stare relegation in the face. Everton won three vital points and were given a useful reminder of just how crucial Wayne was to the side.

Such performances only served to underline the question of how long Wayne would remain a true Blue. Many thought that his astounding ability would outweigh his undoubted loyalty to the club with which he grew up.

The cold reality was that, only a couple of years earlier, the schoolboy Rooney had much to prove – now, it was his club that had to convince their rising star that it was worth staying. Everton might still have to fight relegation. They certainly have little in the way of resources with which to turn around the fortunes and, ironically, selling Wayne is a way out of debt. Even team-mate Tomasz Radzinski was reported to have encouraged him to make a break for it.

It was one of only two real issues that dominated his season. The other might once have been whether or not he might get to go to Portugal for Euro 2004 but, as the year went on, it boiled down to one question – how brilliantly would he play when he got there?

I got the ball, managed to beat a few players and then chip the goalie ... It was one of my first sessions and all the players just looked at me and started to CLAP.

8

PREYING FOR ENGLAND'S LIONS

ENGLAND DEFENDER GARY Neville showed a great deal of perception about Wayne's future. Having played against him in a reserve match, the Manchester United player said, 'I don't think it'll be long before Wayne is with us in the England squad.' His comments followed Wayne's blinding début Premiership goal. Within days, Wayne was asked to join the England Under-19 squad. Before long, he was called up to be a full international.

Since Euro 2004, the country's been full of people who reckon they always knew it was going to happen. It's like all those people who say they saw The Beatles play at the Cavern – if they all had, the venue would have held several million. In reality, few predicted the speed of Wayne's promotion. Barely 18 months before his début, in October 2002, even former Everton boss Walter Smith had been voicing doubts: 'It's been a dizzy rise and, since he's come into prominence, everybody's saying it'll only be a few months before he's going to be an international player. I don't buy that, although I think he will eventually go right to the top.' Come the new year, Smith must have been doing a double-take – along with much of the country.

The England match against Australia on 12 February 2003 was to be all about one man. Wayne Rooney was making his début, setting the record as the youngest player to represent his country. The choice put an end to an extended round of speculation, but it was still a surprise to Wayne's family.

The Rooneys had all hoped that his name would come up, but it was almost too much to believe. As delighted as they all were, they were almost equally shocked.

'When the gaffer [David Moyes] told me I was in the squad, I was really happy,' Wayne said, 'and I asked when the Under-21s had to report. He just laughed, shook his head and said, "No, the full squad." I couldn't believe it. To have the chance to be around senior internationals is going to be a great experience for me and I can't wait.'

The truth was that nobody doubted he was ready; his skill was as apparent on the pitch as his enthusiasm for the game was to anyone who spoke to him. Asked about his own England heroes, his eyes lit up immediately. 'Gazza and Alan Shearer were the main men for me! I used to watch them and they always did well for their country,' he said, 'especially in Euro '96, which is what I want to do myself.'

Wayne was the focal point of a second-half line-up

designed to showcase rising talent. Sven-Göran Eriksson was to field a team of established performers in the first half and then swap them as an entire team for the next generation of footballers. It was a rare opportunity to see an all-new side perform at such a high level, with such fresh under-25s as Francis Jeffers, Jermaine Jenas and Paul Robinson given a taste of the limelight. Eriksson was nonchalant about the youthfulness of the team, including the astonishingly tender age of Wayne himself.

'I'm not afraid of the age of 17,' declared the sage Swede. 'It's more important to see whether he's ready and whether he's good enough. My hunch is that he is.'

From the very first training session, it seemed to be that way. The rest of the squad were astonished by Wayne's blossoming power. 'Well, I got the ball, managed to beat a few players and then chip the goalie,' explained Wayne, as if it were the most obvious thing in the world for a kid his age to be doing against some of the best defenders and goalkeepers the country had to offer. 'It was one of my first sessions and all the players just looked at me and started to clap.'

When match-day finally came around, Wayne Sr chartered a coach to take his friends and family down for the auspicious occasion and it seemed as if half of Everton had joined them down there to wish him well.

'Since he was a little boy, he has only ever wanted to play for Everton and represent his country,' said mum Jeanette. 'I'm thrilled that he has the chance to achieve both his ambitions so soon. Wayne's always been close to all his family and he wants us all there for the game and that makes me just as proud.'

While the family watched, captain David Beckham was there to keep a fatherly eye on Wayne, to keep the press at bay and help out with the young player.

It was a day that crackled with electricity as the crowd strained to catch the first glimpse of England's newest hero. His name echoed around Upton Park as he looked around at the packed stadium with pride. There was so much to play for – not least catching the eye of the England coach – and a young player could do much to assure his future there and then.

The first half did little to enhance the reputation of the old guard. As England failed to pin down the opposing team, Stan Lazaridis took a free kick which found Tony Popovic. He headed past David James to take Australia into an early lead. Michael Owen went on to miss two chances and the Aussies got another one in before the end of the first half, thanks to Harry Kewell. By this point, the subs could not have been blamed for wondering whether Eriksson would even bother to make the swap. But he did.

As the younger team charged out to make an impression in the second half, Wayne showed he was up to the task of maintaining England's glittering reputation. From the off, he made a superb cross to Darius Vassell. Later on, he helped to spread the play out wide to Jenas and this time Francis Jeffers managed to knock in an outstanding cross. England went down 3–1 to Australia, but few noticed the score. The talk was all of the future and Wayne's place in it.

It was only a couple of months before Wayne would make his first start in an England match – and this after

CITY OF LIMERICK
PUBLIC LIBRARY

starting in only ten games for his club side. The match couldn't have been more important. It was the Euro 2004 qualifying match against Turkey held at Sunderland's Stadium of Light on 2 April. The goals were scored by Darius Vassell and David Beckham, but the talk was all of Rooney and his wonderfully impressive full début.

It was a bold decision on the part of Eriksson, who could have stuck with the known quantity of Emile Heskey, to make Wayne such a central part of the team. As it turned out, the Stadium of Light was aptly named, with Wayne as the laser beam cutting through the Turkish team.

Beckham was in trouble before the first ten minutes were up, having been shown a yellow card for dissent. Not long afterwards, he missed a great early opportunity to put his side into the lead – and young Wayne was at the centre of it.

The Turkish goalie had seen off a Steven Gerrard strike and Wayne had had a speculative effort similarly denied. Beckham then narrowly missed a wide-open goal. Turkey continued to dominate the game in the first half, though Wayne surprised even his fans with some increasingly impressive work, particularly just before half-time when he set up Owen. The shot was saved by Rustu Recber.

But Wayne's antics were nothing short of astonishing, including a nonchalant piece of highly skilled ball juggling, followed by a powerful cross that made all those comparisons to England's finest entirely justified. Now everyone could see what a complete player Wayne was, a true all-rounder who could be counted upon in any situation.

It wasn't until 15 minutes before the end of normal play that Vassell scored the first goal, having latched on to a fumble by the Turkish 'keeper after Rio Fedinand's shot. Later still, Wayne fired over from 25 yards, following up some great work by Steven Gerrard.

Shortly before full-time, Kieron Dyer replaced Wayne. As the teenager strode off the pitch, the rapturous crowd gave him a standing ovation and he was visibly moved by the sheer emotion from the staunch England crowd.

Despite a good fight by the Turkish side, injury time saw a great goal from Beckham conclude the match at 2–0. In the after-match interview, Eriksson had nothing but praise for his new team member. 'He's a great talent, we knew that before,' said the England supremo, 'but now we know he's ready for the big matches. I can't see any reason why I should leave him out if he plays like that.'

Back home at Everton, chairman Bill Kenwright was also stunned by what he had seen. 'He's got good vision, he is big, he's strong, he can hold the ball up, he can change pace, he's clever for his age and he can score. If our expectations are high, that's probably good for the boy and will help keep him up there.'

The match reports all agreed that Wayne was a star turn, as he displayed an utter lack of fear against the Turkish defence. Roomania took on new intensity, as it seemed that England might yet qualify automatically for Euro 2004.

The skipper agreed. 'It's a great night for English

football,' said Beckham, adding with a pointed reference to Wayne, 'and for the young players who've come into the team.'

When it came to the first big game of the summer, the match on 3 June against Slovakia, the headlines were all about Wayne. It was another qualifier for Euro 2004, but all anyone seemed to want to know about was what the teenager was thinking and everyone wanted to find out if he was included in the side.

He was, of course, and he made a natural partner for Michael Owen, standing in for David Beckham in the role of captain. It was a tense match, as the visitors went ahead in the first half at Middlesbrough's Riverside Stadium. England came from behind with Michael Owen, who scored the two goals that won the match for England.

Wayne didn't shine quite as brightly as he had on other occasions and was substituted for Darius Vassell before an hour was up. But the excitement in the media around his appearance proved that Roomania was showing no signs of diminishing for the foreseeable future.

The first weekend in September 2003 was a packed one for England sports fans. The country was facing South Africa at cricket and France in the rugby. In football, they were playing Macedonia in a valiant attempt to qualify for the Euro 2004 tournament.

It was an important night for Wayne, who still faced questions about his fitness following his summertime injury in the match against Rangers. Eriksson had witnessed his outstanding comeback performance in the Everton v Charlton match in late August and decided he was ready.

The agony for England in Skopje's Gradski Stadium after a listless first-half performance was compounded by a goal from Macedonia's Georgi Hristov within 25 minutes. The team trudged back on to the pitch, the fans loyally cheering their side, but preparing for the worst. All of a sudden, Wayne took over. Could it be possible that he might be about to shatter yet another record?

The youngest ever goalscorer for England had once been Everton's own Tommy Lawton, way back in 1938. In recent years, the title had been taken by the fabulous Michael Owen. But, on 6 September 2003, Everton were able to reclaim it and their Wayne was the boy whose wide grin confirmed that he knew exactly what he'd achieved.

Michael Owen had already seen Wayne snatch his crown as the youngest player to score in the Premiership and now the young pretender, still more than a month away from being able to vote, showed beyond any doubt that he knew exactly what to do when the opportunity presented itself.

He'd been unusually quiet for the early stages of the game but then, despite all the marvelling over his advanced talent, it had to be remembered that he was still developing. The skill of playing consistently over the whole length of the game, all the time, was one that would come in time. Many other young men of his age were still at school, trying to figure out what to do with their lives, let alone dreaming of representing their country, and it was easy to expect too much.

As it was, barely ten minutes had elapsed of the second half before he made his move. Eriksson had made some changes that everyone was hoping would make all the difference. Best of all, the shrewd Swede had brought on Emile Heskey for Frank Lampard, when some thought he might take off Wayne instead. It was Heskey who received the ball from Beckham, and passed it smartly to the Everton player.

His mastery of technique was spellbinding once again. Not only did Wayne score his first international goal, but it was also an absolute stunner from 20 yards, making the score level. So far from home, in a small Eastern European country, Wayne made a decisive mark in the history books of English football.

Not for the first time, his performance seemed to lift the spirits of the team, as if his youthful passion for the game somehow energised the other players. It turned the game around. Everything was possible and, indeed, Beckham put England ahead after an hour, but, despite his formidable performance and impressive presence, the crowd knew who was responsible for the surge and once again the roar of 'Roo-nee! Roo-nee!' echoed around the stadium.

'To get one for England at such a young age and in such an important game was a special achievement,' Wayne told the *Evertonian* club magazine. 'It's something I'm very proud of.'

Even the normally reserved Eriksson was full of enthusiasm. 'The talent is there, the quality is there with Wayne,' he said. 'Of course, he has a lot to learn, but, if things go to plan, he can go very, very far.'

There was no stopping the boy. The second part of the double-header took place four days later as England took on Liechtenstein at Old Trafford and Wayne played a vital part in a match that was an eerie replica of the tussle with Macedonia.

Established heavyweights David Beckham and Steven Gerrard carried the midfield and battled away against the minnows of Europe, but they didn't make it look easy. That was left up to Wayne, who made up for his inexperience by stamping the bigger impression on the combative Liechtenstein.

They managed to fight off his early attempts, a well-aimed header and a driven shot that went over. And, in coming to the aid of Beckham, Wayne dashed down the left wing to cross in exuberant style to his captain, whose shot then hit the crossbar. An extraordinary overhead kick was his follow-up, but it went over the bar and Wayne had to wait until the second half to hit one home. Even so, anyone following his nimble runs and consistent harassment of the opposition for the first time would have sworn he was a veteran of countless England campaigns.

The first goal belonged to Owen, who headed in a cross from Gerrard with Wayne being involved in the original move. It was a fine way to open the scoring for the match, but the young Evertonian was about to go one better.

Beckham showed his skill as he unerringly picked out Gerrard at the post, who set up Wayne beautifully. The young player's right foot connected superbly with the ball, propelling it with precision into the net and the crowd's cheers were louder then than they would be at the close of play. Gerrard was the first to come forward and rate the man behind the goal he'd helped to create.

'He was magic, absolutely magic,' declared the Liverpool midfielder. 'If he can continue putting performances like that in for us, then we won't go far wrong.'

Wayne was quick to return the compliment. 'It helps a lot having another local lad in the squad and he knows what it's like for me because he was included in the England set-up at a young age,' he explained. 'He's also a quality player, no doubt about it.' In a match which most conceded didn't show England at their best, Wayne's man-of-the-match performance proved that he had enduring star quality.

It was clear that the team were working together well, a testament to Eriksson's skills at ensuring they bonded. He encouraged them to hang out together off the pitch and his relaxed style of management permeated throughout the squad. The players were becoming a close bunch, with Wayne's relative youth forgotten as he quickly found his place at the heart of the England set-up.

They needed all the strength of character they could muster when they took on Turkey in their Sukru Saracoglu Stadium on Saturday, 11 October. It was a crucial match in the run-up to Euro 2004. A draw would be sufficient, but the nightmare scenario was that England might lose and see their automatic qualification vanish.

As if this wasn't hard enough, when Beckham fired a penalty well over the Turkish crossbar in the first half, the home side responded with a barrage of taunts and abuse, much of it from Ozalan Alpay. This was as much a test of Wayne's mettle as anything that had come before in his brief international career – and he showed he could cope well with whatever was thrown at him.

With a solid defence and a team spirit that blossomed in the face of adversity, England showed themselves to be up to the challenge. They played well and Wayne came close to breaking the deadlock when he took a clever pass from David Beckham and fired it over the goal. The draw gave England the solitary point necessary to ensure their automatic qualification into the finals of Euro 2004. And the hot-headed atmosphere in the stadium was another invaluable lesson for Wayne Rooney. If he could flourish there, he could do it anywhere.

With the qualifying rounds out of the way, there were just three friendlies for England to play before the main event kicked off the following summer. Wayne was showing himself to be the revelation that everyone had been hoping for. He was particularly powerful when employed with Owen and Heskey, and the country was expecting the best possible performance from the teenager come June 2004 in Portugal.

They got a taste of what to expect when Wayne opened the scoring for England in the match against Denmark at Old Trafford on 16 November. When he first appeared for his country, he'd had to wait until half-time before he had a chance. On this occasion, although Eriksson made wholesale changes, Wayne was on for more than an hour. And no wonder!

Within five minutes, he put England ahead. He had

powered ahead with Heskey and, after the Liverpool striker was challenged, found some space behind Denmark's defence. Wayne grabbed his chance, and charged in to fire off a rising shot high above the 'keeper, which ricocheted off the underside of the crossbar and into the back of the net. It was his third in just nine matches.

The incredible opening was spoiled only by the speed of Denmark's retort, as Martin Jorgensen scored the first of two goals just minutes later. There was no time to waste and Wayne was at the heart of a set-up from Emile Heskey which he cleverly contrived to get to Joe Cole, who put England ahead again with the third goal of the match in under ten minutes. It was an exchange that was cheered by all England fans, but particularly by Everton supporters, who needed something to celebrate in what was otherwise proving to be a tough season.

That the rest of the match was not so good for England was down in large part to problems with the home team's defence, the weaknesses of which were constantly exposed by the Danes. The Lions just didn't play with enough width to cover their own backs. There were also the unsettling changes at half-time and yet there was still more from Wayne, energetically covering almost every position on the pitch, who saw a stinging effort rebound off the post, luckily for a helpless Thomas Sorensen, before Eriksson sensibly took him off with Beckham, to wild applause. They missed only another goal from Denmark which ended the game 3–2 to the away side.

As far as Wayne's personal performance went, he had

shown invention, style and a cheerleading delight in his game, and had shown the way for his fellow players at several points. Here was someone who repaid fans' devotion and, at times, seemed to be England's only dangerous weapon.

Everton team-mate Thomas Gravesen, appearing with his Danish shirt on, said in the *Mirror*, 'Rooney was frightening, wasn't he? He is amazing. And the most frightening thing of all is that this is just the start for him.'

The last of the friendlies also provided a brilliant morale-boosting performance, as England played Iceland at the City of Manchester Stadium on 5 June. While it was true that nobody really expected that much of the underdog visiting team, England showed the 40,000-strong crowd a side that were at the height of their powers. It was a complete turnaround from the disappointing 1–1 performance in the previous week against Japan at the same venue.

Then the team had seemed lacklustre and Wayne at times had looked bad-tempered and was only fleetingly engaged. What a difference a few days made – even though he was feeling under the weather, he showed that a dose of the 'flu couldn't slow him down.

To begin with, Iceland had a pretty good midfield and, despite an early raid by Paul Scholes which ended in a shot flying over the crossbar, the England side found it hard to make headway. Even Wayne took time to find his rhythm as he paused on a ball from Ashley Cole long enough for it to be intercepted by Joey Gudjonsson. But Wayne kept himself in the thick of the action. When he tried again, it was to see his shot thwarted. Undaunted, he lined up a header which ended up going wide.

David Beckham took a corner which found Frank Lampard free, but the subsequent header also went wide. The Chelsea player turned it around in the 25th minute as he scored with a deflection off the left leg of Iceland's Hermann Hreidarsson which took the 'keeper entirely by surprise. This was where the match really took off and Wayne took centre-stage.

Gary Neville picked up a throw-in just two minutes later and, beating Hreidarsson, smartly worked the ball into Wayne's path. It was all the lad needed to add to England's tally with a textbook shot from ten yards out with his right foot ... and it wasn't his only goal of the match.

Wayne continued to work the crowd with pyrotechnics that saw off three of the opposition with the consummate skill of a world-class player. Barely ten minutes later, he was at his crowd-pleasing best. Paul Scholes – who also shone with his impressive work throughout the match – had knocked the ball back to him and he readied himself with his first touch. He blasted in a deadly accurate shot from 25 yards into the left-hand corner, leaving the Iceland 'keeper helpless and putting England into a 3–0 lead, to the very obvious delight of the home crowd.

As if it were nothing, Wayne wandered away, leaving behind the afterglow of a flash of inspired Rooney genius, having shown how he played from pure instinct and, along with the majority of Sven's other anointed starters, he went off triumphantly at the end of the first half.

There were also two goals by Darius Vassell and one by Wayne Bridge. Though Iceland's Heidar Helguson managed to get one back, the 6–1 result – and the style with which it had been achieved – was just what the fans wanted to see, giving England their first win in six games. It was an exhibition display. What a send-off!

There were exactly eight days to go before England squared up to their first game in Euro 2004 against France. All over Europe, top-class defenders were slowly waking up to the fact that, at some point in the competition, they might need to deal with one of the best-kept secrets ever to play the game. He was young, he was quick … and his name was Wayne Rooney.

I don't see myself as a national hero, whatever anyone has been saying about me. I know who the main players are in the England set-upand I am not there with them just YET.

9

WE COULD
BE HEROES

WHILE WAYNE HAS remained close to his roots, counting two chums from primary school as his closest pals, he's also made new friends among the glitterati of the football world. David Beckham is just one of them. And, while he may be a global superstar worshipped by millions, Wayne insists that, away from the spotlight, the Real Madrid player is simply a good, all-round bloke and family man.

Wayne, the teenager with only a handful of senior games under his belt, eclipsed Beckham at Euro 2004 and, later, the England captain was slated for his performances, especially after ballooning a penalty over the bar in the heartbreaking shoot-out against Portugal.

But Wayne won't hear a word against beleaguered Beckham. 'If I've got a role model, it is David Beckham. He's a lovely man and has really supported me and I want him to be England skipper for years. I only met David a year ago but I definitely rate him as a special guy. He's dead caring, a fantastic person, not at all the way people imagine – he's just normal, just like anybody else.

'Me and Coleen spent time with him and his family in Portugal. It was just like being with any normal mum and dad mucking around with their kids. David's obviously a great dad and I remember thinking, When I'm a dad, I hope I'm the kind of dad like him.

'They're a happy family, really close with their kids and, when me and Coleen have kids, we'd like to be a family like them. I've learned so much being around people like David and Michael Owen. That's why the Euro 2004 tournament could only benefit me, not only as a player but off the pitch as well.

'Everybody can get a bit down if they think their performance isn't good enough. When that happens to me, David whispers a few words in my ear. He's taught me loads, like how to cope with my life off the pitch.

'After the Croatia match, David pulled me to one side and told me he knew what it would be like and what I should expect. He said people I knew would be sniping but said, "You'll just have to forget about it and get on with life."

'I remember, when I scored my first goal for England, I was so excited I didn't know what to do or where to run. David was funny about that, because he'd been there himself. I was telling him about it and he pointed and said, "Well, the England fans are that way, mate," just to skit me. It made me laugh. I'm a bit of a wind-up merchant and it made me laugh.

'Becks is a really good England captain. He certainly knows what he is talking about and deserves to be England captain for years. In these tournaments, it is all about preparation and you see so many little things and pick up so much from him. For example, he told us that when we scored, because it was so hot out there in Portugal and we needed drinks, we should run to the corner flag and walk back so we all got a rest.

'He was always a huge help, having a few words here and there about things. Most of the players are quiet in the dressing room before a game but I speak to the captain and he helps me along. He just tells me to focus and go out there and play my normal game. Most importantly he tells me to enjoy myself.

'All I was thinking about on the pitch in Portugal was winning the game for England. I have got a couple of shirts as souvenirs from Euro 2004. You are given two for each game; I kept one from each game, swapped one with a Croatia player, another with Stevie Gerrard and another one with Becks.

'Those are the ones I really wanted and I've got a designated place where I put all my match stuff – Everton shirts, England caps, England shirts and I've put all the bottles of champagne I've been given in there, too. I've not been tempted to drink them – honest!

'David went over my to my mum after I played for England in Turkey and told her, "You must be the proudest mum in the world." It was a great touch – my mum was dead chuffed, I think she even shed a tear or two.'

Beckham is just as generous in his praise of the young star whom he has helped mentor on the international stage. 'Wayne is an amazing young lad and he performs well even under pressure. He is taking it all in his stride. I'm sure he's been told about all the attention and how to cope, but he just takes playing for England as if he is playing in the schoolyard or Sunday League football. Everybody forgets he is only 18. He plays like a man but he is still a boy.

'Wayne had a sensational tournament, he proved himself in the Portugal competition. He is a world-class player. We are lucky to have a talent like him. People will be talking about him for a long time because he deserves it.

'He's been excellent, everyone knows that. He is a quiet lad but seems very level-headed and on the pitch he is one of the biggest talents. People keep telling me Wayne was ten when I made my England début and that makes me feel old!

'I'm not a jealous person and I'm happy Wayne's getting the attention as he deserves it. Obviously, I've had my share of attention and I'll carry on having it, but it's great for the nation to have someone like Wayne.

'It doesn't feel odd to me at all. It's great that England has got a young talent who is astounding not just the players but the fans. It's great to have players like that for young kids and even older men to look up to. We've definitely got that in Wayne.

'He's got a very strong family behind him. That's what he needs and that's what I've had for a number of years. Without my family and friends, I'm not sure that I'd be where I am now. So I owe a lot to them and he'll owe a lot to his family for being strong behind him.'

Like Beckham, Wayne also suffered his own penalty cock-up for England but, luckily for him, it wasn't in the glare of the spotlight.

The nation's Euro dreams were shattered when Portugal snatched an emotionally charged quarter-final triumph in the spot-kick lottery. By then, Wayne was back in the team hotel with his foot in plaster, after limping off with a broken metatarsal little more than 20 minutes into the game. It spawned a million 'if onlys', after Beckham and Darius Vassell missed from the spot at the end of extra time. Wayne later revealed that he was down to take one of the kicks – yet produced the worst one of his life in practice the night before.

Much was made of a penalty spot that resembled Blackpool beach on that heartbreaking evening in Lisbon. And Wayne certainly had every sympathy with skipper Beckham after his effort sailed into the stand when his standing foot slipped from under him.

Says Wayne, 'I was down to take a penalty. We went training the day before and the players took four or five each. We noticed then that the penalty spot was a bit sandy. It was like, when you put your planting foot down, your foot almost sank into the ground. With my first one in practice, I just scuffed it, not like Becks, but, as I hit it, it just bobbled – I more or less kicked the floor.

'The manager asked at the end of the last training session before the game who would take the penalties if it came to it. I think it was me, Michael Owen, David Beckham, Frank Lampard and Paul Scholes.'

The England player Wayne is closest to is Liverpool's Steven Gerrard. Says Wayne, 'Steven Gerrard is probably one of the closest England players to me, he's a good mate of mine now and, when I first got in the squad, he really helped me. The first thing he did was knock on my door, take me to play pool and made me feel at home.

'Obviously, I get nervous before a game, especially with England, but he really helped me relax.'

When Gerrard first met Wayne, in a Merseyside derby playing for their rival teams, it was angry and ugly. Their infamous confrontation at Anfield in 2002 – a furious flare-up following Gerrard's two-footed lunge on Everton's Gary Naysmith – was a shocker.

Says Gerrard, 'When I first played against Wayne, there was a bit of aggro after the Gary Naysmith incident and he got involved. And, because I play for Liverpool and Wayne plays for Everton, I think people assumed there would be friction between us.

'There may have been a few snarls and a few things said and, of course, when I go out on the pitch for Liverpool I want to stuff Everton – with or without Wayne. But that's normal. That's football and he is the same way.'

The scuffle was soon forgotten and Gerrard was the first to offer the hand of friendship when Wayne tipped up in the England squad. He says, 'The fact is, Wayne is a local lad, he is a Scouser like me and we were brought up in very similar backgrounds. I'm there for him, but he knows about right and wrong. Sacrifices go with any job. The area I'm from, there'd be kids drinking on corners and I had to make sure I wasn't involved.

'Wayne is a good kid and if he needed any advice I'd

help him, but I can't teach him how to play football because, even at this stage, he is one of the best around.

'I realised, though, when he first came into the squad, how he would feel. I first played in the England squad at 18 and know how difficult it was – you don't know anybody and you walk around with a vacant expression on your face.

'You are in awe of some of the players around you. Most of them are older and well established while you are some young scallywag who has just been called up. You come in and you are shy at first. You rarely talk and you don't know what to say. It can be frightening and intimidating.

'You are away from your family and in a room on your own. You may train for one-and-a-half hours but then you have the rest of the day to keep yourself occupied. And, if you are stuck in your hotel room for five or six hours, it can get lonely and boring. You need to get out of your room or you go mad. It is important you make friends and don't sit there all alone.

'That is why I wanted to make sure Wayne didn't feel alone, didn't feel lost and stuck in his own room. I wanted to make sure that he was comfortable. So I just went up to his room and gave the door a knock. I introduced myself and we just got chatting. We got on right away. We swapped a few DVDs and CDs and since then we have had a few meals together. We also play computer games and watch films together. I've really got to know him. He is a great kid and I have got a lot of time for him. We get on like a house on fire. Wayne is quiet with me as well, though. It is just the way he is.

He is not the most talkative lad I have ever met but, the more he gets to know you, the more relaxed he feels.

'I certainly hope Wayne thinks he can rely on me and I like to think I've helped him, just as Michael Owen took me under his wing when I first got into the England squad.

'Wayne's special, the best around. There's ability … and then there is Wayne Rooney.

'He is not as good as people think – he is better. He is different class and he has got it all at such a young age. If you come through at 18, you have done well, but he came through at 16 and that is phenomenal. It is a bit annoying that he plays for the blue half of the city but I would be being a bit greedy to have both Wayne and Michael Owen with me at Liverpool!

'Wayne doesn't need me to look out for him now, we're just mates. He is handling things really well. The only worry is a slight danger that people will expect too much of him. But he is loving the stage, he is confident and I am really happy he produces the goods. There is a lot of pressure put on him, being compared with other players, and people should relax on that front a bit.

'Wayne has already proved in Euro 2004 that he's going to be a massively important player for the future. He is only 18 and, if he looks after himself off the pitch, the world is his oyster. He's very relaxed in his approach to big games and plays as if he has got nothing to lose. Wayne is doing great and, like every Englishman, I hope he keeps it up.

'I think the best advice I gave Wayne is that you don't just get judged on your football, it is how you behave on and off the pitch. It is well documented that I was caught out late four or five nights before an England game. Wayne's got his fiancée Coleen, though; he doesn't need to be going out so much.

'He's matured and he's going to get better. On current form, he is one of the best players in Europe. The experienced England players help him a lot and he has got a good family; he is settled with his fiancée and he is set up to handle the attention the best he can. Thank God he is English! The stage is set for Wayne. He ran the defences ragged at Euro 2004.

'I could go on all day about Wayne because he is a big, big talent.'

Liverpool's Michael Owen is another England star who has become close to Wayne, and someone who has a great deal to lose personally with Wayne's star in the ascendancy – he and Wayne offer Sven-Göran Eriksson an enviable strike force, but, despite scoring against Portugal, Owen was overshadowed by his junior team-mate at Euro 2004. But looking beyond the goal tally, it was the Liverpool striker's selfless attitude, often helping to set up goals for Rooney, which went a long way to helping England's young star to shine.

Says Wayne, 'I don't see myself as a national hero, whatever anyone has been saying about me. I know who the main players are in the England set-up and I am not there with them just yet. Just look at players like Michael. His record at international level is frightening, he has set high standards and he's a really good player.'

Owen himself remembers the moment of magic which almost certainly convinced Sven-Göran Eriksson to unleash the beast in Wayne Rooney on the international stage. England's players were going through their final preparations in the lavish grounds of Slaley Hall in April 2003 when the ball arrived at the Everton striker's feet. What happened next left even seasoned internationals gasping in astonishment and made Eriksson sit up and take notice. Says Owen, 'Wayne got the ball, went past two defenders and just chipped the 'keeper without even thinking about it. All the other players just stopped and clapped him and it looked the clincher for him.

'There is massive potential for us as a partnership, we have different styles and attributes. You can never look too far ahead but there is a possibility we could stay together for England for a long time, maybe the next ten years.

'Age is certainly on our side. Wayne is only 18 and I'm only 24 so we have time to develop a good working relationship. He has vision and awareness and has got strength and explosive pace ... he reminds me of Alan Shearer. He has also got Alan's determination and is difficult to shake off the ball.

'Wayne is a quiet lad and is still finding his way around the international scene. It can be quite daunting to be thrust into a group of senior players when you are at that age but Stevie [Gerrard] took him under his wing and he got all the help he needs.

'I have spoken to Wayne about general things, but not what he should or shouldn't do. He's a striker and there are a lot of similarities to what I've done. And, hopefully, he wants to do some of that for himself.'

One man who has sat down and dished out advice to the new superstar is Paul Gascoigne, himself an Everton player at the time Wayne was rising through the Academy's ranks. If there's one football hero who knows what it's like to be catapulted into the limelight, reducing the profiles of other senior players to mere hangers-on in the media, it is Gazza.

His brilliant performances at Italia '90, where England lost the World Cup semi-final on penalties, made him a global superstar. But the stardom came at a price. He has never been out of the spotlight in the 14 years since and it has taken its toll. Much of it, he admits, he brought on himself. There were times he found it all too much and turned to the demon drink, becoming an alcoholic.

Now, in the twilight of his playing career and still battling the booze, Gazza is acutely aware of the dangers lurking in the shadows for Wayne and has sat down with the lad to share his experiences. Says Gazza, 'So many people have said how much Rooney reminds them of me. I've met him and I like him. He's really down to earth and I hope he goes on to achieve great things. If he learns from my mistakes, he'll be one of the greatest players in history.

'I went on benders at the wrong time and that was my fault. There was lot of pressure from the media and it backfired on me. Whoever you are, you will have your good times and your bad times and I have faced pitfalls. You never know what is round the corner. You think the world's your oyster but you have to be careful about the things that can drag you down. You have to expect the unexpected.

'Wayne can learn from my mistakes. He's a good lad who doesn't need to change anything for anybody. That's what he has to be careful of – changing just because people tell him to and not being true to his roots. He's going to have to learn with every detail of his life being examined. I told Wayne to listen to the people closest to him, his manager, older team-mates and his parents. All I know is that you need your family. They have to stand by you and help you. Even at my worst, my family loved me. They stay with you when others don't.

'I think Rooney and I do share something. We're both fearless. I see it in him. It's what makes him special. I remember seeing him play when he was just 15. Some of the staff at Everton mentioned I should go and watch Wayne. I went to have a look and he was a sub for the Under-19s. He was just 15 but he came on and scored two brilliant goals. I thought, This kid is something else. He has the makings of a great player, a world-class player.

'He should enjoy the attention and the affection but never, never take it for granted. In fact, never take anything for granted. Use the support systems available and be man enough to ask for help. What he has achieved so young has brought back to me the early days in my own career. He has the build of a man, as I had. Like me, he is strong enough and fit enough to handle himself. His upper-body strength is so impressive – and he can finish.

'This boy is our next world-class player. I can see him getting over 100 caps. I wish Wayne all the best. Football is a great life and I'm sure he will make the most of it.

'I don't worry for him because he's full of confidence. I just say, "Be careful." As long as he keeps his head right, he's going to be unbelievable.'

Fittingly, perhaps, the friend whom Wayne respects and looks up to most is closer to home, in the form of Alan Stubbs, his Everton team-mate and the man who took him under his wing as a kid at the Academy. Stubbsy, as Wayne calls him, used to pick the boy up for training and drive him home, and made sure the lad had adequate kit in his Everton locker.

It was also Alan who took a fateful stroll with Wayne along London's posh King's Road, just before Everton's Worthington Cup defeat against Chelsea in December 2002.

The soccer stars, dressed in tracksuit and trainers, decided to browse around an upmarket estate agent – and were kicked out by staff who feared they were burglars casing the £1.5 million homes on offer and threatened to call police!

Recently, Alan took Wayne to his tattooist, Dwainne McGuinness, after the youngster had admired a design Stubbsy had had done two weeks earlier. Wayne, who already sports two tattoos, including his fiancée's name, paid £240 for an 8in Celtic cross to be inscribed on his right arm in a three-hour session at the parlour in Aintree.

Dwainne, 18, who works with his dad Danny, 42, at the family-run business, saysd, 'Wayne didn't flinch and was very friendly, although I was nervous when I realised who he was! He was the perfect client – he sat still all the way through.'

Alan was born in Kirkby, next-door to Wayne's home territory in Croxteth, and the two, once again, are neighbours, this time in Liverpool's millionaire's row at Freshfields, backing on to a golf course in Formby. The duo also share an agent, Paul Stretford, at Proactive Sports.

Father-of-two Stubbs is just 32 but, already, he has fought his way back from cancer – in 1999 he had a testicle removed. He was propelled back to health by a ferocious desire to play football again and, six months later, he turned out for his team Celtic in the reserves. Shortly after that, he was back in the first team.

The soccer star had started out at the Everton Academy but, aged 13, they released him and he ended up playing first for Bolton before he was sold to Celtic.

He came to love the Scottish team but, 14 months after his first op, he suffered a relapse, prompting his move to Everton for the sake of his family, wife Mandy and their children, Heather, eight, and Sam, four, who had missed their friends at home.

He flourished at the club but then, in 2002, disaster struck again and the player needed a tumour removed from the base of his spine. Again, the star's indomitable spirit saw him fight his way back to health – and the pressure-cooker of the Premiership.

But it also gave him a philosophical approach to life, taking one day at a time and putting his family above all else, an ethos he explained to rookie Wayne as he rocketed to stardom.

Today, the pair are good mates, popping in and out of each other's home and Alan is always on the end of the phone when Wayne needs some sound advice. 'He's a right pest!' Alan jokes. He told the *Evertonian* magazine, 'I think Wayne's got the potential to be one of the best we've ever seen in the country. It was a tough season for him because he's a marked man. Every reporter in the country is waiting to knock him down. He's only 18 and he basically carried the hopes of a nation on his shoulders, along with Owen and Gerrard.

'I think he's been absolutely fantastic to come as far as he has done in such a short space of time. It's great that he looks to have a level head on his shoulders, he's not soft and I think he's doing everything right at the moment. He's just got to be careful now because he's there to be shot at, but I think he's coped brilliantly.

'There's nobody with more admiration for him than me and his Everton career has been great, he's an idol amongst the fans – and still only 18!'

Wayne says simply, 'There's an age difference between me and Alan, but I'm probably closer to him than any other player. He's a great bloke, a good laugh and, to me, it's people like Alan who are heroes.'

IT can be difficult, but what 18-year-old wouldn't want to be doing what I'm doing DOING?

10

TEARS OF A CLOWN

IF THERE WAS one word which emerged to chill the blood at Euro 2004, it had to be 'Wazza'. The England camp had apparently decided to nickname their brilliant new talent after an old one – Gazza. While it might have amused them, neither Wayne's agent nor his sponsors were smiling. Quite apart from the fact that the word 'wazz' is slang for urinating, the spectre of Gazza's squandered talent has loomed ominously over Wayne ever since he first blazed into the headlines.

Mention of Gazza and Wayne in the same breath was inevitable, since nobody could fail to notice the eerily striking similarities between the two most precociously gifted English players of their generations.

As with the similarly stocky and bullish Gascoigne, Wayne sometimes seems to have experience beyond his years on the pitch, which helps explain their shared fearless attitude to football – neither of them are awed by their own talent or physicality, and especially not the opposition. Both come from solidly working-class families, fed on a diet of sausage and chips, their mothers both working as cleaners to make ends meet while each of their dads worked as labourers on building sites.

Those families, extensive and herded together on the same council estate, are both clannish, proud and, inevitably, prone to spats.

Wayne's relations have been known to trade a few booze-fuelled punches, notably at the do for Wayne's fiancée Coleen, just like Gazza's before them – his dad often offered to thump people, even outside the family who feuded, fell out and kissed and made up with unerring regularity.

Both are thick-set, with the look of a bulldog, 5ft 10in and around 12 stone with a tendency to run to fat. Just like Gazza, Wayne has already been criticised for his weight and come out fighting, declaring, 'I'm not going on any diet, I need to keep my strength up.'

The two were both talent scouted, failed academically, got into youth teams at a young age, scored goals for Everton and stole the international limelight with sensational performances for England.

They even look similar, with an edgy, macho ruggedness born of the mean streets and we're unlikely to ever see either don a skirt outside of a fancy dress party.

Emotionally, they are alike as well – Gazza's tears at Italia '90 captured the soft centre of a nation, his raw, artless sentiment touching the primeval, parental core at the heart of even the most hard-bitten and cynical.

Wayne, too, is unafraid to wear his heart on his sleeve, talking with unabashed frankness about his love for Coleen, shedding tears after the ruckus at her eighteenth-birthday party and displaying an intense, protective loyalty towards his family.

As far as the cynics were concerned, the scene was set, the script already written – Gazza had morphed into Wazza and it was only a matter of time before another backstreet hero would bite the dust.

But Wayne has cast aside the script, refusing to be pigeon-holed and determined to be himself. He may be just a boy of 18, still rough around the edges and caught between the transition from teenager to manhood, but he has so far handled the spotlight with startling aplomb. His TV appearances have been measured and modest. Unlike others, who often run away at the mouth, Wayne says little but what he does say is thoughtful and designed to defuse difficult questioning.

Challenged on Michael Owen's performance immediately after an England game, he refused to rise to the bait, swerving criticism of his strike partner, saying, 'Michael is a great player. The goals will come.' Enigmatic Sven couldn't have done better himself.

Neither has Wayne been caught on drinking binges or carousing with celebrity pals around luxury hot-spots. The most daring paparazzi shots of Wayne so far have merely shown him enjoying a canoodle with fiancée Coleen on a Barbados beach or hobbling to his car in the moon-boot which protected the metatarsal injury to his foot, sustained during the Euro 2004 tournament.

He was also pictured engrossed in a book –

Gascoigne's recent autobiography *Gazza: My Story*, in which the fallen star bravely confesses his mistakes and offers timely advice to youngsters following his hallowed footsteps on the pitch.

Wayne's passion for the game – one which Gazza unquestionably shared – has so far remained untarnished by the love of celebrity which Gascoigne embraced so whole-heartedly from the moment his World Cup tears made him a paparazzo's dream and manager's nightmare.

Unlike Gazza, Wayne appears to have the mental strength and discipline to understand that his good fortune depends on his performance on the pitch, as well as off it.

His cartwheel celebration at Euro 2004, after scoring the first of two sensational goals against Switzerland, was an impulsive, welcome display of his joy, one which will have been copied on thousands of school pitches up and down the nation.

Contrast that with Gazza, who embarrassed the nation by choosing to celebrate his stupendously skilled goal against Scotland at Euro '96 by sprawling on the turf and miming the guzzling of drink.

As a role model, and now a national hero, Wayne recognises that his behaviour will be scrutinised every inch of the way. Despite the fact that he was sharing a relaxing holiday alone with Coleen at the exclusive Sandy Lanes Hotel in Barbados after Euro 2004, he happily signed autographs and posed for snaps with children who surrounded his sun lounger.

He also knows that he is living a dream. 'It can be

difficult, but what 18-year-old wouldn't want to be doing what I'm doing?' he replied, when questioned about the pressure of stardom. No whingeing, just a straightforward acceptance that he's lucky and that sacrifices go with the territory.

It was in stark contrast to Gazza who, while he was complaining to the talkshow host Terry Wogan that he was exhausted after the 1990 World Cup, and had been granted a reduction in his early-season training schedule at White Hart Lane, was involved in modelling shoots and recording the excruciating 'Fog on the Tyne'.

Of course, there have been slips and embarrassments along the way for Wayne. Police investigated complaints from Liverpool fans that he spat in anger towards opposing supporters during a bad-tempered match in April 2003. Wayne had been taunted by Liverpool supporters during the derby match and was alleged to have spat on the pitch in front of them. If it was deemed that the alleged spit could have upset someone, Wayne could have been charged under a public order offence.

The incident was one of a series of unpleasant episodes during the match, which Liverpool won 2–1. Two players were sent off and a red headband was painted on the statue of the Everton legend Dixie Dean at Goodison Park. A memorial at Anfield to the people killed in the Hillsborough Stadium disaster was also daubed with paint.

Police took no action against Wayne after studying video footage of the incident but, as the youngest player in the Premiership to have ever been sent off, it was clear that the opposing fans had hoped to spark a fit of temper in the star which would get him into trouble.

And the childish, insulting taunts so beloved of opposing fans on the football terraces have also begun – 'He's fat, he's Scouse, he'll come and rob your house … Rooney, Rooney …' is just one which already resounds round the grounds.

But these minor irritations are less important than Wayne's own reaction to the escalation of his fame. At the moment, he's playing it cool, growing into his public persona by simply being himself.

There will, inevitably, be more slip-ups on his journey to the stratosphere of world football, but Wayne's own strength of character will determine how many and how severe they are.

Unlike Gazza, Wayne is not crippled by the need to please others; he feels no need to be a joker in the pack, no need to be a crowd-pleaser when he's off the pitch. He'd rather please himself and does, choosing to spend time with his family and lifelong friends, rather than swanking around at celebrity haunts.

He shunned booze for mineral water during his £600-a-night break in Barbados and opted for quiet evenings at the hotel restaurant with Coleen rather than wild nights out clubbing.

Wayne also has the kind of self-awareness and self-esteem which the brilliant, tragic Gazza always lacked. It wasn't booze which destroyed Gazza, but what drove him to it – the depressions which started in childhood, panic attacks, obsessive behaviour, all were demons that tortured his soul.

There's no doubt Gazza was, like Wayne, in love with the game; he just didn't love himself nor, poignantly, did he even know himself, confessing recently in his autobiography that he knew how to be Gazza, the media-star, but never how to be plain Paul Gascoigne, the breathtakingly gifted footballer.

Gazza, the boy who wanted to be loved at any price, fell in love with the alluring siren of fame at any price, even infamy; that's what proved more toxic than booze to his career in the end.

But Wayne is lucky that lessons had been learned from the dissipation of Gazza's once-dazzling talent before the boy wonder's name had even been chanted on the terraces. Wayne has been cosseted and protected in a way Gazza never was. It begs the question – if Gazza had had the same support network around him as Wayne seems to have, how much more could he have achieved in a career that offered so much, but seemed to come off the rails so often?

The Everton manager David Moyes famously spent two years growling like a lioness over a cub, shielding his protégé from the media spotlight and refusing interview requests with all the ferocity of a Wayne Rooney tackle. It was a wise tactic which allowed Wayne to be groomed and grow in confidence in a way dear old Gazza never was.

Wayne didn't receive his first media baptism until May 2003, attending his first ever press conference and, a month later, when he did the same for England, he took Steven Gerrard with him for support.

And Wayne is also protected by a ring of steel in the

form of Proactive Sports, headed by his powerful agent Paul Stretford, a man with more than 120 Premiership players on his books.

Says Stretford, 'There is no doubt Wayne has the potential to earn an awful lot of money and there is always the risk that could take away some of his hunger for football. But I really don't see that scenario happening with him. Wayne loves his football and that is the main drive in his life. He wants to achieve and become one of this country's best players and won't be diverted from that by anything – or anyone.

'People are going to put temptation in his way and there will be distractions in his life, both close and far from home. The making of him is how he handles them and that is why we are here to help him. He is very caring and generous around his family but he is not stupid with his money. Things are being set up in such a manner that he never will be. He is very aware of the need for investment and he will not take all his money and blow it.

'A major part of our work so far has been having to say "No" as far as commercial offers are concerned. We are taking a long-term view. In the first instance, there will be four or five long-term partners. They will be blue-chip brands. It is very difficult to quantify what he will be worth. I have the remarks of one agent, who is the antithesis of what we are trying to do. He claims Wayne has become worth so many millions overnight. But we are not looking for that quick hit.

'He will be carefully managed for the next 20 years. The sky is the limit but it will be done in a controlled manner. I am not going to put a headline figure on it but the deals we are talking about will be substantial and record-breaking both in size and length of term. We have this philosophy about Wayne which will present him as the real thing. We have launched a trademark brand and called it "Rooney – Street Striker". That's what he still is. That's where he learned to play his football from morning to night. If he didn't have a ball back then, he used to kick a Coke can around.

'The life change he and his family have had to contend with is cataclysmic. His progress has been like a volcanic explosion. That has a lot of plus sides but the downside is that he is a young lad who will make mistakes.

'Wayne seems shy when you first meet him, although those who know him best will tell you he is anything but that. One of his biggest assets is his mental ability to cope with things. Little fazes him. Let's not forget that he didn't leave school long ago and there has been a massive change in his life. But he knows who he is and what he is about. He also has a close-knit family. They are a lovely, genuine family. Wayne won't become a brat because of them. His mum answers all his fan mail and is very switched on, the powerhouse of the family.

'I really hope the nation as a whole recognises that in Wayne we have a real treasure who should be cherished. We should all be proud of him.'

The most disturbing aspect for Wayne is not that the goldfish bowl of superstardom will make his every move transparent, but that his family, who never asked for fame, will also be subjected to the same intense interest. He says, 'My family are just ordinary people and they didn't ask to be in the spotlight.'

He and Coleen have been sparing in their public appearances, preferring instead to lie low with friends at their Formby home and shunning the multi-thousand-pound offers that pour in every day from media worldwide.

The couple agreed to one magazine photo shoot, on the occasion of his splendid eighteenth-birthday party at Aintree racecourse, but promptly donated the £100,000 fee to Liverpool's Alder Hey Hospital, where Wayne has become patron of the Rocking Horse Appeal.

Wayne has since satisfied the public's lust for Roomania with a series of newspaper interviews. Having spent time with both Wayne and Coleen, I can testify to Wayne's surprising good nature, shrewd mind and warm wit. There was none of the surliness, shyness or taciturnity for which he'd become reputed; rather, once he'd taken stock of the situation, Wayne was full of light-hearted banter, happy to send himself up with self-deprecating humour and was refreshingly honest in his replies. He was also surprisingly eloquent, in contrast to the way he had been portrayed – and often described – as a lad 'who could barely string two words together'.

It's fair to say he has a little way to go before he'll acquire the polish which will prevent the absurd sniping and sneering of middle-class commentators – about a tie undone here, gum chewed there, but he's a quick learner ... blimey, he didn't even open his Coke bottle with his teeth!

It's often said that Gazza's career was prematurely ruined by self-indulgence, but his career statistics are those of a wonderfully gifted footballer who fully deserved the attention and adulation he received for his brilliance on the pitch – 19 years of top-flight football, eight clubs, 457 appearances and 110 goals, as well as 57 caps and 10 goals for England, including one of the best goals ever scored in the European Championships, and he was still playing in the Premiership at 35. Sad, then, that he is perhaps even better remembered by many for his booze binges, pranks, belching and wearing false boobs ... now there's a stark warning for Wayne if ever there was one.

THE party was great, but handing over the cheque was the best bit – it was a brilliant way to celebrate my eighteenth, I was really made up. To be able to do something like that is a privilege and I don't forget THAT.

11

BRAND NEW

THE PLAYERS FROM Greece went home after winning Euro 2004 in a bus bearing the legend 'Ancient Greece had 12 gods – Modern Greece has 11'.

In Britain, though, there was only one – Wayne Rooney, the fleet-footed champion whose chariot was already filling with gold before his plane touched down on the Heathrow tarmac.

Wayne's sponsorship deals have already netted him a £10 million fortune but his sizzling performance at the Euro 2004 tournament has begun a scramble among marketing men which has the potential to earn the 18-year-old more than ten times that amount. Says his agent Paul Stretford, 'Provided he stays fit, Wayne has the potential to earn upwards of £100 million over the next decade or so. We're emphasising that, unlike Beckham, we won't be preoccupied with fickle fashion.

Wayne's the real thing, an amazingly talented street footballer who can appeal to every kid in the world.'

Before the soccer sensation had limped off the pitch after the injury to his foot in the match against Portugal, his £2 million Nike contract was already under re-negotiation, and was eventually upped to £5 million over ten years. The star will also net another haul of cash from performance-related bonuses as part of the deal, the biggest sponsorship contract for any teenager in the world. Nike UK spokesman Simon Charlesworth said, 'In the eyes of a number of commercial partners, Wayne is more valuable now than when the tournament started.'

Added to the Nike deal is a £500,000 deal with Coca-Cola, a £500,000 contract to act as ambassador for Mastercard and a £1.5 million endorsement deal with car giant Ford. A further deal with a telecoms company is in the offing.

Max Clifford, one of the world's leading PR gurus, says, 'Everything depends now on his performance on the pitch – and how he handles the media. If he has good relations with the media, it will comfort sponsors. It could make a £50 million difference to his commercial value over the next five years.'

Clifford, whose offices are in London's posh New Bond Street, has represented huge names like The Beatles, Muhammad Ali, OJ Simpson and Simon Cowell, as well as many famous brands. He adds, 'Rooney is still an unknown quantity. He has a reputation as being feisty on the pitch. It is not yet known how easily he might be wound up off it. The

CITY OF LIMERICK PUBLIC LIBRARY

relationship his advisers have with the media will decide how any slip-ups are dealt with. If Rooney is not carefully handled and his image controlled, it can make big-name sponsors very nervous.'

Clifford, who also represents Beckham's alleged lover Rebecca Loos, adds, 'Sponsors do not want to invest millions and millions of pounds in somebody who has a poor relationship with the media because it backfires and can reflect badly on them. That is what I believe has happened with David Beckham in recent times. I know that, had Beckham been my client, the Rebecca Loos story would not have needed to emerge. In my view, the whole sorry saga was badly handled and, as a consequence, Beckham's form and status has suffered.

'I have spent 35 years running my own PR business and one of the most important aspects of managing any client is to know what they're up to, to anticipate any problems and to deal with them before it all gets out of hand. You can only do that by having a solid, healthy relationship with your client built on mutual respect and trust.

'I remember, some years ago, an agent coming to me and asking if I would handle an up-and-coming sports star. He expected me to work for nothing, because the sportsman was going to be a big name. The star was Paul Gascoigne and I turned down the contract over a salt-beef sandwich with his then agent Mel Stein. I don't believe I could have helped save Gazza from himself. What I do know is that I could have helped save him and his family from some of the worst spats they all suffered with the media.

'That would be my caution to Rooney – to make sure he has advisers who can help him and his family develop a good, healthy relationship with the big names in the media early on.'

Wayne's star has also risen in the East, where he has eclipsed Beckham as the number-one foreign pin-up in China, just as he eclipsed the iconic idol on the pitch at Euro 2004. With a population of 1.3 billion rapidly falling in love with football, China is regarded as potentially the world's biggest football audience and merchandise market.

Even before Euro 2004, Wayne was well known in China because Everton is sponsored by Kejian, a Chinese telecoms company, and one of Wayne's team-mates is Li Tie, one of China's top footballers. Everton even has its own website in Mandarin, visited by more than 500,000 people a day. On 1 January 2003, more than 330 million Chinese tuned in to watch the live Premiership action between Everton and Manchester City, despite the time difference meaning that the game kicked off after midnight.

But, since Euro 2004, Wayne has risen to become China's pre-eminent foreign hero, with shops selling out of shirts bearing his name – which translates as 'silly nun' in Chinese – within a hour of his first goal hitting the back of the net.

The Chinese widely praised Wayne's aggression on the pitch, contrasting it favourably with Beckham's more manicured style. Gong Lei, the coach who briefly brought Gazza to play in China in 2003, says, 'Football is a man's game and Rooney always scares his rivals even if he's still a child. Beckham may be a pop idol but it's usually girls who prefer him to Rooney.'

Internet chat rooms overflowed with praise for Wayne and the National Sports Bureau in China even invited him to the 2008 Olympics in Beijing. Ha Haiyun, a reporter at the *Titan* sports paper in China, says, 'Here, if you like stars, you choose Beckham. If you like football, you choose Wayne. He has shown real signs of character and we like that sort of person. His fearlessness is his most appealing quality.'

Beckham is currently believed to earn £15 million a year in endorsements off the field from sponsors including Adidas, Vodafone, Pepsi, Marks & Spencer and Police sunglasses. A tour of the Far East with his pop star wife Victoria and a charm offensive in America were designed to woo two of the world's biggest emerging football markets while playing up his sex appeal as a fashion icon and image as a devoted family man.

But it all went horribly wrong when ambassador's daughter and PR girl Rebecca Loos alleged that she'd enjoyed an affair with Beckham, and tawdry text messages between the two were splashed across the world's media. Overnight, the Beckham bubble burst, his star seeming, if not actually to plummet from the sky, to waver slightly and perhaps shine a little less brilliantly – a new hero was needed.

Step forward Wayne Rooney, in dazzling style, a lad who captured the very essence of schoolboy dreams – a working-class boy from the cash-strapped backstreets who'd honed his craft with a crumpled Coke can, ripped trainers and a burning desire to succeed.

He may not have had the face of an angel nor the body of a model, but Wayne had a raw charm all of his own; there was magic in his boots and unmistakable manliness in his soul – at last, a real *Boy's Own* hero.

Birmingham City's managing director Karen Brady says, 'If not quite the invisible man, Beckham, the world's most desirable bloke, relegated himself to Mr Anonymous in Portugal. If the Rebecca Loos affairs weakened Beckham's hold on the family audience, the responsibility for his collapsed status as the hero who performs last-gasp miracles rests on the shoulders of Wayne Rooney. For Beckham, 2004 is the equivalent of the year The Beatles split up, the year Margaret Thatcher was told to go and the year that Gazza thumped Sheryl. The end of the affair with a worshipping public. Now all eyes are elsewhere – on Rooney.'

Roomania also gripped the rest of the nation. At one pub in Clifton, Bristol, takings went up by 90 per cent during Euro 2004 after landlord Fred Aylett turned his Roo Bar into the Rooney Bar and barbers reported a sudden surge of boys asking for Wayne's simple haircut. At Scissor Kicks in Liverpool, a football-themed barber's, queues formed. Hairdresser Kenny Flynn says, 'The style is pretty much a straightforward short-back-and-sides – Number 4 on the top and a 2 on the side. It's a typical Scouse haircut – and it cost just £5.50.'

Fans besieged Everton's souvenir shop, clearing the shelves of the number 18 shirt worn by the star and DVDs showing his goals. The shop has since been forced to employ more staff and to remain open three hours later to cope with demand. A spokesman at the

Everton megastore said, 'We've sold tons of Rooney stuff – I've never seen a frenzy like it.'

And rich fans clamoured for the chance to live next door to the star in Liverpool's exclusive Formby, bidding up to £3 million for a new, seven-bedroom mansion being built on a plot beside Wayne's home – a similar pile which cost him £900,000 when he bought it.

Developer Michael McCoomb said, 'We've been inundated with enquiries since people heard of the Rooney connection – and many have landed serious offers. Roomania has created a massive interest in the property. Wayne and his fiancée Coleen are a lovely couple, really down-to-earth. They often stop and chat with the builders.'

Wayne's square face is already so iconic that the artist Peter Blake included it in a recent reworking of his Beatles *Sergeant Pepper* album cover.

But any suggestion that Wayne will topple Beckham as a lifestyle icon is premature. His agents, Proactive Sports, are looking to capitalise on Wayne's allure as a Bash Street Kid who blasted his way to stardom by practising his skills on street corners, rather than creating a manufactured, glossy image. Says Stretford, 'Wayne is a product of his environment – the streets and the terraces. He is not manufactured, he is a real person and I don't want him to lose that appeal.'

Jon Smith, chief executive of First Artist Corporation, a leading sports marketing agency with 250 footballers on its books, believes there's room in the market for both Beckham and Wayne. He says, 'Rooney and Beckham are not the same product – they can both comfortably cohabit in the sponsorship marketplace. Rooney has a sporting appeal, whereas Beckham is both sporting and lifestyle. But Wayne's proved he's a big game player who seems to revel on the big stage. If he sticks to endorsements from a few blue-chip companies strongly affiliated to football, he will do very well. The working-class background will be the making of him.'

It's a view shared by leading PR analyst Mark Borkowski, who has worked with everyone from Gorbachev to Maradona and whose brand client list now includes Vodafone and Smart Car. He also believes Wayne can learn from Beckham's mistakes. He says, 'Rooney doesn't have the natural film-star looks yet which gave Beckham universal appeal – his fans are almost undoubtedly mostly boys. Boys grow into men and the challenge for Rooney is to keep those fans with him. The public loves a wry wit and Wayne's natural sense of self-deprecating humour will prove endearing, the public will buy into that.

'But he needs to remember, above all else, that it is what he does on the pitch that will govern his popularity and marketability. His biggest asset is himself ... if he remains true to himself he will remain a valuable marketing commodity. One of Beckham's problems has been that he bought into himself as a commodity – he began believing his own hype. It looks like Becks is quickly becoming just another burned-out celebrity and he doesn't deserve it. Maybe he has his advisers to thank for that. He needs to get back to his roots and playing football. Becks can still be a god on the pitch and he must now blaze for his last professional challenge – the 2006 World Cup.

'Rooney also needs to recognise he has a responsibility as a role model and to give as well as to receive. Beckham lost sight of the fact that he was a role model. He became so "St Tropez bling-bling", he failed to recognise that every time he had a new hairstyle or a new tattoo millions of ordinary kids would be clamouring for the same or getting into trouble at school for sporting inappropriate hairstyles or fashions.

'The cult of greed enveloped Beckham and it all became about dosh, dosh, dosh with little thought for the chaotic effect his ever-changing styles would have on the pockets of ordinary families.

'Beckham also became remote and inaccessible – every interview he gave had to be on his terms, he was rarely seen to be helping anybody to anything except himself to large sums of money. He surrounded himself with a PR army who took the view, "They need us, David, we don't need them." That is unwise, especially because, at some point, relations always sour.

'Whether you are forgiven a mistake by the public is very often governed by the way you are perceived to have behaved; if you've been high and mighty, you are much less likely to be given a break.

'Rooney is already patron of a hospital charity in Liverpool, helping sick children and raising cash for an appeal there. That gives him substance and shows he is trying to use his fame for the good of others, too. He can further manage his brand by sticking to a few, big, reputable sponsors who he can grow and work with over a number of years.

'Beckham has many sponsors but one of the most successful relationships has been with Vodafone; it has allowed him to grow without succumbing to the whims of fashion which change so very quickly, leaving a celebrity looking tired and jaded.

'Above all, what Rooney must do is serve the game. That's what Beckham forgot.'

Bronwen Andrews is director of Ketchum Sports Network in London, a leading agency which has a prestigious client list, including two associated with Beckham – Pepsi and Adidas. She believes Wayne has sparked a trend, in which football is going back to its roots in search of working-class heroes. She says, 'The enormous support for Rooney has not come from marketing him to the fans, but from the grass roots. The fan base was already there, before Rooney became a household name. That is thanks to his talent, and it is his talent and consistent performances on the pitch which will give him credibility and increase his value. Football is a trendy sport but Rooney has down-to-earth appeal and he also has youth on his side. What has been interesting from our perspective is that the tremendous surge of support for Rooney is based on the fact that he is a working-class boy, with tremendous talent, in contrast to other players who are more showbizzy.

'Everything goes in cycles with the media and it seems the public finds Rooney a refreshing change from the very glitzy way some footballers have been marketed in the recent past. Rooney, as he is now, could easily be used to market family and youth brands. It's not difficult to imagine him in an advert for something like baked beans, for example – he already has that kind of youthful, family-based appeal.

'He needs to be careful not to become too heavily marketed or promoted and to concentrate his efforts on his football – as with all soccer stars, he is largely only as good as his last performance on the pitch.'

THERE is nothing like scoring for your country – it's a great feeling. Scoring goals for your club is fantastic but, when it's England, the feeling is **UNBELIEVABLE.**

12

CROWN PRINCE OF EUROPE

THE ATTENTION OF the sporting world was fixed on Portugal in the early summer of 2004. It promised to be a dramatic beginning to a season of action that would reach its peak with the mighty Olympics that were to be hosted by Greece in Athens over much of August.

And the summer of sport got off to an amazing start as Wayne turned in a performance of Olympian standards all on his own. In a storming Championship, he put in three all-conquering performances and racked up four goals for his country, before injury saw him hobbling off to take a well-deserved break.

Rarely had a build-up seen the hopes of an England Euro squad based around one such fresh talent. But with his presence virtually assured in every game, preparations for the fourteenth tournament were well under way.

When the European competition first started, a quarter of a century before Wayne was even born, the inaugural finals were held in France. It wasn't until 1968 that what had been called the European Nations' Cup became the UEFA European Football Championships. This was the year that host country Italy won a replayed final against Yugoslavia 2–0.

The tournament's biggest changes came in the 1990s, when the fall of Communism meant a united German team played, as did the former states of the USSR. In the memorable England-hosted Euro '96 Championships, far more teams competed than ever before, thanks to the continued emergence of former Eastern European states. There, Germany won with a golden goal against the Czech Republic, and France took the title in 2000.

The matches in Euro clashes became recognised around the world as some of the best in football. It had become a huge spectacle with an impressive global audience. Such was the skill of the sides involved that some looked to the four-yearly engagements as being more exciting than even the World Cup, where the talent could be more variable.

Though the tournament has seen its fair share of drama and controversy from the start – such as Greece's refusal to play Albania in 1964 when the two countries were on a war footing or the exclusion of Yugoslavia during the Balkan conflicts of the early 1990s – few Championships have reached the level of excitement and anticipation in England than when Wayne flew out from England with his team-mates.

The side arrived in Portugal on the back of a satisfying

qualifying campaign, topped with the 0–0 draw against Turkey back in October 2003 from which they earned automatic qualification. Only the first match against Macedonia, in October 2002, had been disappointing, with the 2–2 draw which could have led to Turkey gaining the coveted slot. Wayne performed well in the match at home against the Turks which England won 2–0 and the team went on to win the following three qualifiers before they drew again in Istanbul.

Of the side that went out, Wayne says, 'The squad seems a lot more solid these days than it was six years ago or whenever. Even if we get injuries, there are great players to come in and take the position – that gives us a great chance of going to Portugal and winning.'

It was an incredible pressure to shoulder, but Wayne's clear-eyed gaze and carefully chosen words gave no sign that he was daunted by his responsibility. 'Personally, my first aim was to get selected and then to make the starting 11,' he says, going on to reveal his ambition by only then adding, 'There is nothing like scoring for your country – it's a great feeling. Scoring goals for your club is fantastic but, when it's England, the feeling is unbelievable.'

On the cusp of the tournament, Wayne received the backing of none other than footballing legend Sir Geoff Hurst. 'He's an exciting young talent and one who has to be nurtured properly. But can he do well in the European Championships? Yes, he can. There's no limits to what he can do.' But the former England ace sounded a note of caution. 'A major finals is very different to regular internationals, but he can handle it.'

All over Europe, people were taking notice of Wayne Rooney. Spain's Fernando Morientes was one of many to comment that the Evertonian and his Liverpudlian strike partner, Michael Owen, were likely to work together very well. 'Owen is a very good player and important for the way England will play. He is the goalscorer in the team. Owen is still young but he has been ready for tournaments like this since he was 18.

'He will be able to help Rooney if they are playing together. Rooney is young but I have seen how strong he is and he plays like a man. Owen can use his experience to help. They will be a strong partnership for England because together they are strong, have pace and will be difficult for defenders to stop.'

Wayne put his good relationship with Owen down to Eriksson's skill in his role as boss. 'Michael likes to play on the shoulder a lot more, while I like to drop in and that suited us both. But that comes down to Sven just telling us to go out and play our normal game. He is like that, it relaxes us and most players are happy to do that.'

Everyone back home was as aware of the scale of the mountain that the team had to face. The best that England had done in the Championships so far was to reach the semis in 1968 and 1996.

The opening match for England was against France in Lisbon on Sunday, 13 June. Wayne knew the importance of the task ahead for the team and for him personally. In a career that could only be described in superlatives, this was his biggest game by far and he could hardly hide his excitement at getting stuck into the challenges to come. 'We believe we can do it. Every time I have met up with England the squad is bouncing. We really want to win and we have a great chance of lifting the trophy,' he said. 'We know our opening match against France is a massive game. If we beat them, it will be a major boost and victory would give us a great chance of going all the way.'

Over in the French camp, the opposition knew only too well that England would be anything but a walkover. Their coach, Jacques Santini, had no doubt that the game would be a tough one – and Wayne would be one of the ones to watch. 'Rooney has the capacity to explode at this tournament in a very big way. He has a goalscoring instinct that could set him apart from the others in Portugal,' admitted Santini. 'There are always two or three players who stand out at these tournaments – and Rooney could be one.'

Not that the Frenchman wished that Wayne didn't do well. 'I just hope that he becomes very good from the second match onwards and not before then! We watch him regularly. He's full of daring, freshness and spontaneity – and that is a very dangerous combination for us.'

Dangerous Wayne revealed the secrets behind their warm-up routines that gave him that freshness and spoke about how England psyched themselves up. 'We all know everyone at home is behind us and, when we are out on the pitch warming up, there are always a lot of shouts like, "Let's do it for the fans." The feeling is unbelievable because you know the whole nation is watching and cheering you on.'

The Lions represented a real challenge for the French

and were a team to watch as all the countries sized one another up in the early stages. 'England will be one of the favourites for the tournament. The beginning of the competition will be a big test for them because they have to play France,' said Fernando Morientes. 'In that game, we will see how good England can be – what they are capable of.'

The match took place in Lisbon's Estadio da Luz before an expectant crowd eager to see a titanic struggle. There was a frisson of excitement as the French strode out, particularly the unmistakeable figure of Thierry Henry. This was someone who had particularly earned Wayne's respect.

'He's some striker!' exclaimed Wayne in a pre-match interview. 'He's different to all the others I've seen over the last few years. I think he's the best striker around – and there are plenty of good ones. France are a great team with great players.'

The admiration was mutual, as Henry openly spoke of his regard for the young player.

'He's a young talent and really special. And he always scores special goals,' remarked Henry. 'He does it even more for England – and it should be more difficult. International football is another level and sometimes you can be paralysed. How many players do you know who are outstanding for a small club and can be amazing for the national team?' Perhaps Henry might be forgiven for referring to Everton as a 'small' team – undoubtedly, Everton fans will have ample opportunity to remind him of that as Henry visits Goodison in seasons to come.

When kick-off for England's opening game of the European Championships finally arrived, France were unable to threaten David James or the England goal as the defence held up and the team played a tight, measured game, despite the searing heat of the Portuguese afternoon. Wayne managed some superlative holding action and it all paid off with a goal by Frank Lampard before 40 minutes had elapsed.

David Beckham had cleverly crossed to Lampard, who slammed home a powerful header past a nonplussed Fabien Barthez. This was quite some achievement, the first goal any team had scored against France in 11 games. The vocal English fans roared their approval.

At half-time, the England team dashed from the sweltering pitch into the dressing room to take much-needed ice baths in an attempt to restore some energy to their tired muscles.

After play resumed, France managed to get themselves back into the game. Patrick Vieira picked out Henry, but, though he curled a speculative shot towards the England goal, it was saved by David James. Just as artful as the Arsenal player's attacking runs was the ferocity and sheer determination of Wayne's running off the ball and his link-up play. He never let up as the French tried desperately to contain him.

Michael Owen was replaced by Darius Vassell as Wayne continued his one-man assault. In the end, it was Mikael Silvestre who stopped him in his tracks, tripping him up in the box and receiving a caution – and a penalty award – for his pains. Beckham took the penalty, which was saved well by Barthez diving full length to his right.

It was all the French needed to inspire them in the final quarter of the game. Emile Heskey, who was subbed when Wayne went off in the last 15 minutes, was pulled up for a foul near the edge of the England box and Zinedine Zidane curled a stunning free kick past James. Zidane and Henry were suddenly unstoppable as England gave away the second penalty of the match, when Steven Gerrard inexplicably chose to pass back to James, whereupon Henry intercepted the pass and surged into the box. James could do little else but bring the French legend down. Zidane, the French captain, stepped up to take the penalty, and buried it mercilessly.

The dispirited Lions trooped off the pitch as the French went on a lap of honour to celebrate their victory. It was little comfort that they'd easily put on a fantastic display against one of the best teams in the world, or that Wayne had performed admirably in a high-pressure international match. Revealing further misery, Wayne later claimed that Claude Makelele 'tried to wind me up. He was standing on my foot, standing on my heel and all that. It's sad that a player of his talent needs to try to get someone booked or sent off. When people try things like that, it just makes me want to beat them more.' It was a positive attitude towards adversity mirrored by fans who quickly got over their disappointment to ensure football and Roomania held equal sway for the next few days back home.

On 17 June, England played their only game outside

Lisbon. It was the second group game against Switzerland in Coimbra, with a 5.00pm kick-off. This was to be the match in which Wayne provided the impetus for England to show that they could do everything their fans hoped for. The circumstances couldn't have been more difficult.

Forget the Swiss; the real enemy was the roasting heat. It was early evening in the UK and cooling, but in the Portuguese stadium the temperature never dipped under a sweltering 30°C, just over 80°F. No amount of training can prepare players for a full match under those sizzling conditions and yet it's so often when the going gets really rough that England deliver.

It didn't look that way to begin with, as the side could barely keep possession of the ball. The Swiss were storming forward, with danger-man Hakan Yakin busy exposing the weaknesses in England's defence. In the boiling atmosphere, Wayne soon succumbed to hot-headedness, taking on Lampard's pass and lunging at the Swiss goalkeeper in a move which earned him a yellow card. His antics confirmed his reputation for being an edgy player, someone who completely lacked cruise control. He just piled in there, in a way that had earned him warnings back home with Everton. Minutes later, the tangle became unimportant as he completely redeemed himself.

As he later recalled, 'It came after a good run from Stevie Gerrard, who gave it to David Beckham. Becks pinged it to Michael Owen and he just chipped it on my head from six yards. I couldn't miss. As it was against the run of play, it gave us a bit of relief.'

Shattering yet another record, the star headed the ball straight into the net, becoming the youngest player to score in a European tournament. Bringing a cliché to life, Wayne literally turned cartwheels with delight in front of the crowd.

'I have no idea where the cartwheel came from!' he later admitted. 'It was just a reaction. I don't even know why I did it.'

Back home, Old Stanley Arms landlord John, from Old Swan in Liverpool, knew exactly where the impromptu gymnastics had come from. 'The first goal against the Swiss meant a lot to Wayne. You could see it written across his face and that cartwheel was great to watch. It was like he was saying to the world, "I've arrived, take a good look."' It was, he added, a measure of how important the goal was to Wayne that he let his delight overcome him. 'Wayne's very accustomed to scoring. He has always scored goals and I think he only tends to celebrate when it's a really vital goal. Otherwise, he just regards it as a job well done when he bangs one in the net and walks away calm as you like. Wayne's a very modest lad, he's never been one to show off about his success.'

The goal had a dramatic effect on his lacklustre team-mates, who then managed to create a couple of opportunities, with Owen and Wayne at the centre of them, before the half-time break.

After an inconclusive performance for much of the second half, Wayne popped another one in at the expense of 'keeper Jorg Steil. From Owen Hargreaves to Darius Vassell, the ball was set up for Wayne whose shot smacked into the post and rebounded off the goalkeeper to give England their second goal and effectively breaking the Swiss resolve completely. It wasn't a bad day's work at all, albeit not necessarily played at the level it could have been, and Wayne left a few minutes later, just after Gerrard brought the final tally to 3–0. It was a professional job, nonetheless.

This was the game that was to blast the Roomania firecracker into the stratosphere, with unbridled adulation exemplified by the *Daily Telegraph*'s cautionary article on cartwheeling. The day after the match, the Royal Society for the Prevention of Accidents (RoSPA) was quoted as warning fans not to try to imitate the gymnastics Wayne performed after his goal, in case they sustained injuries. 'Fans have always copied crazy celebrations but the Rooney cartwheel could cause injury if not done correctly,' a doom-laden statement warned.

Now, this was undoubtedly true. Despite any jibes about his size, Wayne was a trained athlete at the top of his game. And yet, the idea of a nation cut down by a wave of foolish cartwheels instigated by a teenage footballing genius was as good an indicator as any of how far Wayne had moved on from being a mere player. He was a genuine phenomenon.

He was also a deserved Man of the Match and his boss spoke warmly of him – the teenager was a manager's dream. 'I'm not surprised he's the man of the day, not only in England but in all of Europe,' said Eriksson, 'being an 18-year-old and playing football like he is doing and scoring goals. I think he'll be even better in the future. He can improve still, I'm sure about that. I've had many young talents in the past – Rui Costa, Roberto Baggio and Paulo Sousa, but I think Wayne Rooney is the best. He is something very special – I must say he has been absolutely fantastic.'

So often compared to the likes of Paul Gascoigne for his bravery and unpredictable gung-ho attitude to the game, it was perhaps only to be expected that the man himself would join in with his own view. 'He gets better with every game,' said Gazza. 'If he keeps playing like this at Euro 2004, he'll get the same reception coming home that I did after Italia '90.'

Wayne himself was quick to highlight the contributions made by the other members of the side. 'We have got a good squad and a good bunch of players, so this is no one-man team, no matter who it is,' he insisted. 'It is not all on me, it is about the other players as well. I think the team were a bit nervous, but once we got the goal we settled down a bit, and when we got the second we were a bit more relaxed and knew we were going to win the game.'

And he was quick to quash the rumblings of discontent surrounding Michael Owen's performance. Perhaps, some queried, the pair were too alike to play together for England? 'I don't feel any sympathy for Michael because I know it won't be long before he's banging in the goals again,' said Wayne. 'He's a great player and I'm sure he'll be back on target for England very soon. He set up my first goal against Switzerland and I'm sure he's happy that we won the game, even if he didn't score.'

CITY OF LIMERICK PUBLIC LIBRARY

England had a long weekend to think about and prepare for the match with Croatia on which all their hopes of quarter-final action were pinned. Wayne had the extra burden of knowing that a yellow card in the next game would result in him missing the quarter-finals. And, although he vowed not to moderate his game in order to get through the match unscathed, the rest of the team were praying that he would be around to make his vital contribution to their continuing efforts. England without Wayne Rooney had somehow become unthinkable.

It was back to the Estadio da Luz in Lisbon for the crucial match against Croatia. Michael Owen managed to worm his way behind the Croatian defenders in the first couple of minutes, but, when he crossed to Wayne, it was just too high for his strike partner. Within what seemed like only a few seconds, English hopes turned cruelly to disbelief as England went behind after six minutes when Niko Kovac scored from close range. Croatia needed only to defend that scoreline to ensure their safe passage through to the quarter-finals.

Fully aware that another goal by the Croats would probably be fatal for England's chances of qualifying for the latter stages, the team nevertheless swept relentlessly forward. Wayne continued to be a midfield dynamo, eventually threading a ball through to Paul Scholes, who managed only to find the 'keeper.

As half-time loomed, it looked as if the nightmare scenario would materialise, but David James managed to get behind an effort by Dado Prso, marking a turning point in the match.

Minutes later, Wayne got into a good position near the Croatian goal-line and lofted a cross to Paul Scholes, who instinctively headed home from close range to even the score. England were on their way back at last. And then, just to give everyone something to talk about at half-time, Wayne scored again.

'Paul Scholes squared it for me,' he said, 'and I just hit it as hard as I could. Goalkeeper Tomislav Butina got a hand to it but I think the power took it past him. I thought it was in when I struck it; the ball swerved a bit, he did get something on it, but it still went in.'

England were ahead and Wayne was once again the hero of the hour, and the relief on the faces of the English players as they marched off for a well-earned break was all too evident.

In the second half, England seemed far more confident and they needed to be, as the Croatians were not giving up. While the Lions had hesitated in the game against the Swiss, there was a much more satisfying cut-and-thrust this time around. Wayne set up Owen, who only just missed scoring his first goal of the tournament. The roles were reversed after an hour elapsed. As Wayne received a fine pass from Owen, he slipped the ball nonchalantly past the Croatian 'keeper.

'My second goal in the match was probably my favourite,' he later revealed. 'Michael Owen played it straight into my path just inside their half and I ran on with only the 'keeper to beat. I looked up into the right-hand corner of the goal and their 'keeper dived a bit early, so I just rolled the ball in the other corner. I only decided where to put it as I ran towards Butina, before celebrating with Scholesy.

'That goal probably gave me the greatest pleasure, because when it went in I knew, more or less, that we had qualified for the quarter-finals. I didn't know where I was running to after I scored, it just happened. The crowd was so loud and you just don't know where you are going.'

Incredibly, it was his fourth goal since arriving in Portugal and, his work more than done, he was taken off five minutes later, to a standing ovation from the England supporters who were euphoric. Wayne himself has been quick to point out that he still has so much to learn – after his performance against Croatia, it is hard to imagine what that could be.

Although the Croatians pulled another goal back, Lampard retaliated and the game ended 4–2 to a jubilant England. The team were through to the quarter-finals!

Back home, Roomania was sweeping the country like a tidal wave. He was front-page news everywhere and there wasn't a pun on 'Roo' or 'Rooney' that wasn't used several times over – 'WE'RE THROO', 'LET'S GO ALL THE WAYNE', 'OUR HEROO' … and there are several hundred even worse than those. But the greatest praise came from gaffer Eriksson himself. Not a man given to gushing, his comparison of Wayne to one of football's greatest ever exponents of the art showed just how highly Wayne was rated by his fellow professionals. 'I don't remember anyone making such an impact on a tournament since Pele in the 1958 World Cup,' said Eriksson. 'I am a little frightened about comparing

Rooney to Pele because of the pressure it will put on him. But, when someone like him scores four goals in three games in a tournament like this, you can't stop it. So far, he's kept his feet on the ground – and that's the only worry for the future.' Praise indeed, and it could only be topped by a glowing tribute from the master himself. The Brazilian was only too happy to oblige: 'Wayne Rooney has already emerged as one of the best players at the European Championships,' said Pele, interviewed at an engagement in London. 'I just hope that he is allowed to remain focused on his performance and that the only pressure he has to carry is that which he puts upon himself.'

Speaking of the different world in which the young pretender was playing, he said, 'There is certainly a lot more pressure on a young player. It is something Wayne will have to learn to cope with. In less than a year, he has grown up tremendously and would now be a serious candidate for anyone's current list of the world's greatest living footballers.'

Back home, Wayne's family were not surprised. As far as they were concerned, it was just the rest of the world catching up with what they already knew. 'I first started telling people about my sister's son many moons ago,' says Wayne's uncle John Morrey. 'Wayne was only about 13, but I was going on at everybody I knew, telling them to remember his name because he was going to be a very special footballer.

'The passion he displays on the pitch and the inspiration he can be to his team-mates puts him in the same class. Pele was a magical player who loved the game and you can see that in Wayne every time he treads on the turf. He has the power to change a game with a single kick of the ball and that is what separates good players from the greats.'

Just three days later, England took on the host country in the quarter-final that the world was talking about. At home, people all over the land stopped what they were doing to watch the game – even the organisers of the mighty Glastonbury festival put up screens as thousands of music fans put rock 'n' roll on hold for footy that Thursday evening.

It turned out to be the night Wayne's Euro hopes came to an end with the injury that was so reminiscent of the one that had been such an upset for Everton fans in the friendly against Rangers the previous summer. With England fans on their best behaviour, the focus of the Portugal game was entirely on what happened on the pitch. At 7.45pm it started so well for Eriksson's men, as David James launched a huge clearance upfield, which Costinha misjudged, allowing Michael Owen to take advantage and make for goal. He immediately sized up his options, clocked the goalkeeper off his line, and brilliantly flicked the ball with the outside of his right foot over the 'keeper's head and into the back of the net. Not to be outdone for the entire tournament by his protégé, Owen broke another record of his own, becoming the first Englishman to score in four consecutive international tournaments. Three minutes in, and England could not have dreamed of a better start.

But Portugal fought back fiercely and it seemed difficult for the Lions to get a grip on proceedings.

English backs were to the wall as wave after wave of Portuguese effort was thwarted by staunch defending and solid goalkeeping. Then disaster struck. Only 20 minutes had elapsed when Wayne was clipped by Jorge Andrade, losing a boot in the process. The referee then inexplicably decided to penalise the England player.

'That annoyed me more than the injury at first, the fact he gave a free kick against me,' Wayne later recalled of the decision, going on to say of the aftermath, 'There wasn't like an instant pain. I didn't feel anything when I ran with my boot off, it was only when I put it back on and put a bit of weight on it. That really started to hurt.'

After hobbling back, he sank to the ground before he reached the halfway line. Confusion reigned, as it seemed at first he had a twisted ankle. Bravely, he came back on to try again, but it was clear he could hardly bear his own weight on the damaged foot. Although it had looked as if he would have a massive impact in this crucial winner-takes-all battle, it signalled the end for young Wayne. He limped around for a while before conceding defeat and making his exit from the game and it was later announced that, like his captain before him, he'd broken a metatarsal in his foot.

Having been replaced by Darius Vassell, Wayne's absence became, worryingly, all the more significant. The boy wonder was as much a lucky charm for the side as he was a player and the Portuguese team seemed to sense it. In the 20 minutes or so on the pitch, Wayne had forced a save by shooting from an awkward angle, but the triumphs of previous games were now impossible. In his absence, Owen switched to link up play, intending to feed the marauding Vassell, and the pair caused some concern for the Portuguese defence as attack and counter-attack flowed up and down the pitch for the rest of the half.

England managed to hold on to the lead until minutes before the end of normal time when Helder Postiga equalised. Dramatically, Sol Campbell thought he'd given his team victory minutes later, but the goal was disallowed in another controversial decision when the referee awarded a free kick to Portugal against John Terry for impeding the goalkeeper. As the game went into extra time, each side managed to score another goal, forcing the clash to go to the dreaded penalties at the end of what had otherwise been a fine encounter.

The first penalty set the tone for what was to be a night of deep disappointment for England – Beckham's ballooned shot over the bar delighted the home supporters, but put extra pressure on his team-mates to remain in contention. Although Portugal missed a penalty late on, the result was almost inevitable – England's Euro 2004 journey eventually shuddered to a halt as the team went down 6–5.

It was painfully reminiscent of the team's previous best showing, in 1996, when they went out on penalties in the semi-final against Germany. The difference was that ten-year-old Wayne Rooney had watched that match at home with his family and now, just two tournaments later, he was out there sharing the agony with the rest of his team on the pitch, or at least near it.

'I could only watch from the team hotel, I couldn't do anything about it,' he later said of his frustration. 'We know anything can happen in a shoot-out and, unfortunately, we went out. It would have been unbelievable to have finished as the leading scorer but, to be honest, I would have traded all my goals to win the tournament.'

As Euro 2004, with its triumphs and disasters, faded into memory, Wayne spent time recuperating from his injury, facing up to the possibility of missing the opening of the new season. Meanwhile, negotiations soon got under way between his representatives and Everton and all sorts of inducements were reported in the media. Would he play for Everton again? Would he be a Manchester United or Chelsea player next season? Or would he join Ronaldo at Real Madrid?

His scintillating skills on the pitch were undisputed. How he goes on to cope with the siren-call of fame and the intense glare of the spotlight will, at the end of the day, be the real test of his strength of character. It has often been here, rather than on the pitch, where so many other bright young talents have tripped up.

And what next for the boy wonder? Despite Everton's alleged offer of £50,000 a week, a club record, the lure of fabulous riches and playing among the élite of the world's footballing talent may prove too much for Wayne and, perhaps more significantly, his advisers. It's clear where his heart lies, but his future is infinitely more obscure. Evertonians may have to accept that, sooner or later, the lad they have invested in, nurtured and supported from the age of 11 may not be in a position to repay the club with his breathtaking talent on the pitch.

Everton director Paul Gregg observed on the BBC's

Five Live in the aftermath of the European Champion-ships, *'From Everton's point of view, this is home-bred talent who has not had a chance to mature with Everton Football Club. I think we all feel that we've not had the full benefit of his talent to date. I sincerely hope he will still be here when the season kicks off, but unfortunately it may be other forces which make those decisions for us.'*

Whatever unfolds in the months and years to come, while it might be possible to take Wayne out of Everton, no one could take Everton out of Wayne, the club he has breathed, eaten and slept since the day he was born. And, while there might be some soul-searching over an eventual decision to leave, he'll undoubtedly have a special place in the hearts of all true Blues ... and the feeling will be mutual.

For another who eventually left Goodison, albeit in the twilight of his career, Gazza's story acts as a morality tale of woe and poignant 'if onlys'. In avoiding a similar fall from grace and a terrible waste of a wonderful talent, Wayne could do worse than to remember another *If* – and that's Kipling's. Give or take a few minor alterations, these sentiments from the nation's favourite poem could well have come from the mouths of any of Wayne Rooney's mentors so far, as well as the ones who'll guide the nation's favourite teenager in years to come:

If you can keep your head
When all about are losing theirs and blaming
it on you ...

If you can force your heart and nerve and sinew
To serve your turn long after they are gone ...
If you can talk with crowds and keep your virtue,
Or walk with Beckham – and not lose the
common touch, If neither foes nor loving
friends can hurt you;
If all men count with you, but none too much,
If you can fill the entire 90 minutes
With a complete game's worth of distance run,
Yours is the Earth and everything that's in it,
And – which is more – you'll be a Man, my son!

CITY OF LIMERICK PUBLIC LIBRARY

35030

CHRONOLOGY

24 October 1985   Wayne Rooney was born –
                   Everton had just enjoyed their
                   most successful season ever,
                   winning the First Division
                   Championship and the
                   CupWinners' Cup.

1994   Aged 7, Wayne's first proper
                   match for the Under-12s at
                   Storrington; he came on as a sub
                   and scored.

1996/97   Scores a record-breaking 72
                   goals in the Liverpool Primary
                   Schools League.

1996   Wayne joins the Blues Academy.

20 November 1996	A proud day, as Wayne comes on as Everton mascot in the Merseyside derby at Anfield.
2001	As his career begins in the Everton Academy, Wayne scores eight goals as the team makes it to the FA Youth Cup.
September 2001	Comes off the bench in the Under-19s Merseryside derby to score the winner with the last kick of the match.
15 December 2001	As a newly signed Academy scholar, Wayne appears before an ecstatic crowd at Everton and asserts his determination to do well for the team.
April 2002	Leaves De La Salle School.
20 April 2002	Sits on subs bench in 1–0 Premiership win against Southampton.
17 August 2002	Makes his full Premiership début for Everton at Goodison Park against Tottenham Hotspur.
14 September 2002	Booked for the first time as Everton win 2–1 against Middlesbrough.

1 October 2002

Making his scoring début in the Premiership, Wayne gets two goals in 3–0 win at Wrexham in the Worthington Cup, the youngest Everton scorer.

19 October 2002

The classic opener, Wayne scores his first Premiership goal in 2–1 win over Arsenal. He becomes youngest player to score in a Premiership match at 16 years old, and his last-minute, 25-yard strike also ended the Gunners' 30-match unbeaten run.

8 December 2002

Wins the BBC Young Sports Personality of the Year award, presented to him by Sven-Göran Eriksson.

26 December 2002

Becomes the youngest ever player to be sent off in the Premiership when he sees red against Birmingham City.

17 January 2003

Signs his first professional contract with Everton until 2006.

12 February 2003

Making his England début in a friendly against Australia, Wayne is the youngest player to represent his country at 17 years and 111 days when he replaces Michael Owen at half-time. The previous record of 17 years and 253 days had been set by James Prinsep in 1879. England lose against the Aussies 3–1.

February 2003   Signs a new and improved contract with Everton that earns him £13,000 a week until 2006.

2 April 2003   Man of the Match in his first competitive start for England against Turkey in a Euro 2004 qualifier at the Stadium of Light.

August 2003   Passes his driving test at the third time and is handed a SportKa worth £9,995 with the number plate R00 NI as part of his sponsorship deal with Ford.

August 2003   Chosen by England coach Sven-Göran Eriksson as 2002/03 England Young Player of the Year.

6 September 2003   Breaks Michael Owen's record to become the youngest ever scorer for the Three Lions when he registers his first England goal aged 17 years and 317 days in a

Euro 2004 qualifier in FYR Macedonia.

13 June 2004	Euro 2004 tournament begins with a match against France, which England lose 2–1.
17 June 2004	England v Switzerland, Municipal Stadium, Coimbra – England win 3–0, with Wayne scoring twice.
21 June 2004	England v Croatia, Estadio da Luz, Lisbon – England win 4–2, with Wayne scoring twice again.
24 June 2004	England v Portugal, Estadio da Luz, Lisbon – Wayne limps off the pitch after 20 minutes with a broken metatarsal; 2–2 after extra time, Portgual win on penalties 6–5.
25 June 2004	The speculation over whether Wayne will stay at Everton starts in earnest.

WAYNE'S WORLD OF FASCINATING FACTS

Robbie Williams was forced to cancel a party performance for Rooney's eighteenth birthday and engagement to fiancée Coleen McLoughlin due to scheduling problems.

Rooney was named Britain's favourite Scouser in a poll of 2,000 people outside Merseyside. He polled more votes than Beatles George Harrison and John Lennon, who were third and fourth respectively. Sugababe Heidi Range came second.

Rooney now holds an account at Coutts, the posh bank where the Queen keeps her dosh.

Rooney is planning to launch a single with bad boy rapper Mark Morrison – but his favourite crooners are soulboys Lionel Richie and Usher.

His dad, Wayne Sr, is a pigeon fancier – and gets on famously with Wayne's boyhood hero and Everton star Duncan Ferguson, who shares his passion, and keeps a loft of 25 pigeons at his £1.2 million mansion.

It cost £8,500 for Wayne to insure his first car, a Ford SportKa.

He's nicknamed The Duke by Everton fans because they reckon he swaggers like John Wayne.

A third of men would rather kiss Rooney than a host of top glamour models, a survey revealed. An incredible 36 per cent of the 1,500 men who took part in the *Zoo* magazine survey said the player would be top of their list. Actress Kelly Brook and model Nell McAndrew were second and third!

Wayne Rooney is now the most searched-for male personality on the Internet according to Virgin.net.

A talent agency scouring the country for Rooney look-alikes to take part in a new TV show had a few problems. London-based firm Juliet Adams said, 'People who look like David Beckham are happier to go into the modelling business, but men who look like Wayne Rooney tend not to be such poseurs.'

A baby sea lion has been named after Rooney at the Welsh Mountain Zoo in Colwyn Bay, North Wales, and a kangaroo at a North Yorkshire sanctuary.

Bookies started taking bets on a boom in babies to be christened Wayne in 2004. In the previous year, just 43 boys were given the moniker. Sporting Index offered spread bets on 250.

The Radio City radio station in Liverpool changed its name to Radio Rooney for one day after discovering it was the star's favourite.

Rooney has been dubbed 'The Baby Bomber' in Italy, and 'The Messiah' in Spain.

Rooney has a tattoo at the base of his spine which reads 'Then'. It was his first, done as a lark with a mate, who has one at the base of his spine which reads 'OK'. The duo were constantly ribbed for being inseparable and ending every sentence with 'OK, then.' Each had one word inscribed to have the last laugh.

Football-mad mum Diane Coathup was the first to add Rooney's name to that of her new-born son. Everton-mad mum-of-seven Diane, of Prenton, Merseyside, christened her 5lb 7oz tot Michael Wayne Rooney Coathup. Mum Kerry Masters, of Beccles, Suffolk, named her tot simply Rooney Masters, believed to be the first to use the star's surname as a Christian name.

Rooney became the youngest player ever to score in the European Championships in 2004 – and more than 17 million tuned in to watch, over three-quarters of the male TV audience.

Rooney asked England goalkeeper – and accomplished cartoonist – David James to sketch his beloved chow Fizz from a snap he carried in his wallet while they were in Portugal.

Rooney has been adopted by the Chinese as their number-one pin-up – and nicknamed 'Baby Elephant' because of his mixture of 'charm, tantrums and occasional clumsiness'.

His surname, found mainly in Ireland, dates back to the thirteenth century. A genealogy website states that Rooney is the anglicised version of 'O Ruanaidh', from 'Ruanadh', a personal name meaning 'champion'. The principal family with that name originated in County Down.

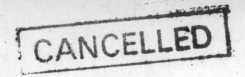